# Incredible War Stories of WWII

9 Women Who Helped Win the War

**Nel Mead**

# Table of Contents

# Introduction

*The use of women agents became a game changer during WWII because of their ability to infiltrate enemy lines undetected.* –Giles Milton
*Expert advice quoted from 'Churchill's Ministry of Ungentlemanly Warfare'*

The historical books on the Second World War, like every war, will focus mostly on the strategies and leaders operating on history's grand stage with large armies clashing on the battlefields. Nevertheless, this is an incomplete image. In reality, wars have always been extremely complicated, especially in the modern era, involving entire societies and nations with a great amount of activity in politics and economics.

Living through a disaster brings things to a place where logic and reason are secondary to what is necessary to survive. Looking back at history, we know the outcome of all these efforts. We cannot make judgments of individual's efforts because we are completely removed and detached from the brutality and reality of the war situation they tried to manipulate and survive. We can say that women have always participated in wars in any way they could, to help their nations and their countries win. This fact is often forgotten and overlooked. Unfortunately, we had to watch two bloody wars in quick succession to remember the cost, courage, and commitment of those involved.

All of us are connected to our country's destiny, like it or not. Women have always known this but in recent times, that truth has been forgotten. The purpose of this book is to remember what it took to win WWII and the essential contributions made by a few women who sometimes gave their lives for the cause.

In the following pages, we will discuss the stories of nine extraordinary ladies who used their talents and abilities to help the Allies win the war against the Axis. Before that, in the first chapter, we'll provide a historical overview of the period, and the role women spies and agents had in general. Also, the reasons and the demand for their participation in the war effort.

Then, we'll see the story of Nancy Wake, an example of loyalty, along with resilience and courage, developed in the face of challenging and heartbreaking childhood years. She was an independent woman, capable of escaping capture and adapting to new roles. A feminine woman with the strength of a true warrior in battle, she remained strong and even personal tragedy couldn't break her spirit. In chapter three, we'll talk about the story of Virginia Hall, an acute strategic mind and a tenacious woman who got a higher education and insisted on seeking more active and important roles in diplomacy and war than her personal circumstances allowed at the time; the fact that she had a wooden leg after a terrible accident didn't stop her from having an impact on the front lines. Then, we'll see the tragic story of Noor Inayat Khan. She was a sensitive and dreamy young writer who followed Mahatma Gandhi's pacifist ideals. Still, the sense of duty to both her countries, Great Britain and India, made her decide not only to support the Allies' effort in her writing but also to enter the battleground physically. She is one of those who gave their life for the cause presented in this book.

In the fifth chapter of the book, there is the story of Pearl Witherington, the only woman to lead a network of Special Operations Executives (SOEs). Beginning as a courier, she displayed such determination, resilience, and organizational skills that her contribution became crucial in maintaining the resistance and offering help to the Allies during D-Day and beyond. Then follows the chapter dedicated to Krystyna Skarbek, who provides another lesson on adaptability and resilience in the face of aversions and transformations. She was a woman who had the tenacity and courage to take over dangerous missions, such as negotiating the release of prisoners successfully, thanks to her quick thinking and determination. The next chapter presents the story of Vera Atkins, a woman of strength and commitment to justice whose organizational abilities and dedication proved critical. Of a cosmopolitan background, her skills made her enormously more important for the SOE than her formal position as a non-British citizen allowed.

Then, we'll discover the story of another woman of a cosmopolitan background, Violette Szabo. A spirit of adventure and bravery, she was courageous and tenacious even after her capture and imprisonment by the Nazis. She is another one of those who gave their life for the victory, indomitable and committed to the end. Chapter 9 tells the story of Amy Elizabeth Thorpe. This is what everybody expects when hearing about women spies: the seductive spy. But she was much more than charming. Coming from a high society background, ties with political and military environments, and relationships with foreign diplomats, she was the right person to influence influential people and obtain crucial intelligence. Our stories about brilliant and resilient women who offered a lot to the war effort against Nazism close with the story of Andree Borrel, another woman who gave her life fighting for her country. A real patriot, capable of receiving rigorous training and completing clandestine missions, she is known for her fearlessness and resolve, which made her face arrest and imprisonment by the Gestapo. She maintained fortitude and bravery until her execution.

A legacy of courage, patriotism, adaptability, insistence, commitment to the victory over the Axis, and sacrifice—that's what this book is all about. The stories of nine women who can symbolize millions of others, women and men, who gave everything they had, from the positions they were in and with the abilities they had at their disposal, for the Allies to win the most crucial war of modern history, the one that permitted our societies to exist and evolve the way they have.

# Historical Note:

# The State of the World Leading Up to WWII

The causes of major wars, but also wars in general, are always complex. Political tensions and economic issues often play crucial roles in the outbreak of wars, which was undoubtedly the case with World War II. First, the devastating results of WWI, which at the time was called "The Great War." Millions died, mostly the young, and production and international trade shrank after decades of rapid growth. Second, the Spanish flu added to the death count. Those years decimated the European youth of the time. On top of everything, the Great Depression, a decade later, created a period of economic instability and great difficulties for many Europeans and Americans.

We mentioned pre-war trade and economic growth. A growth that, before the war, had made many intellectuals and politicians think that maybe wars were a thing of the past; delusions that were tragically destroyed with the massacre of 1914-1918. Nevertheless, the experience of WWI did not make everybody wiser. On the contrary, the horrors of that war led many to become even more naive than before. During the 1930s, while Hitler and the Nazis were preparing to launch another great war to erase the negative outcome for Germany of the previous, many in Europe and America thought that arguing against the "war" in general and promoting pacifist ideals would resolve the problem and the danger which they refused to acknowledge.

At the same time, Germany was devastated economically due to the war and the Treaty of Versailles of 1919, which imposed heavy war penalties on the nation. There was high unemployment, hyperinflation, and social unrest; Hitler began his political career advocating erasing the treaty's arrangements and the treaty itself. Then, in 1929, the Great Depression followed, making everything even worse and creating an even more favorable environment for *Nationalsozialismus* or National Socialism (Nazism), to rise.

In fact, the rise of German nationalism began even earlier and was only accelerated by the harsh economic conditions, which we can say added the socialist element and made it rougher and more aggressive. Moreover, it was not only a German phenomenon. During the previous decades, an additional two new great powers had similar political and ideological development and friendly relations with Nazi Germany: Italy, which had expanded their colonies in Libya and Ethiopia, and imperial Japan, which had colonized a great part of Eastern Asia, including Manchuria in China. Their goal was that the world should no longer be dominated by the British and their young cousin, the USA, along with the French and the Russians, who had, in the meantime, become communists and Soviets. This wasn't about the economy, international trade, and diplomacy but world domination and there was only one way to achieve that—war! We are witnessing something similar again after the Russian invasion of Ukraine.

Germany, Italy, and Japan became increasingly militaristic during the 1930s. While the French and the British wished they could avoid another great war, the Americans had returned to their seclusion, and the Soviets had funded one of the most brutal dictatorships in history during the Stalin years. In 1938, Hitler began implementing his expansionist project with the *Anschluss*, that is, the occupation of Austria. Britain and France continued to appease him, as they were afraid of a new war and cultivated the naive hope that by conceding to Hitler's demands, they would satisfy him and make him stop pursuing further expansion. Of course, it was exactly the other way around. Appeasing an aggressor emboldens them and makes them even more aggressive. World War II is the best lesson for the real and dangerous consequences of pacifism: it could never convince the aggressor to become peaceful, and instead, it only weakens the peaceful and makes it easier for the aggressors. Nobody could be more helpful to Hitler or today's and future aggressors than those who think peace comes from imagining or wishing and not from being strong and ready to fight against them.

The Munich Agreement of September 30, 1938, was the peak of the appeasement, as British and French leaders Chamberlain and Daladier agreed on conceding Sudetenland, the Western region of Czechoslovakia, to Germany to maintain peace. Crowds cheered for Chamberlain at the airport when he returned, thinking of him as the savior of peace. In reality, the Nazis were just preparing for the real deal.

Less than a year later, on August 23, 1939, Nazi Germany came to an agreement with the Soviet Union as well. On September 1, the German troops invaded Poland, followed a couple of weeks later by the Soviet troops from the East. Britain and France finally understood the mistake and declared war on Germany on September 3. It was the beginning of World War II, which would pass through many different stages, with a series of conflicts in various regions of Europe, North Africa, East Asia, the Atlantic, and the Pacific, with former allies becoming enemies and unlikely alliances giving way to earlier rivalries.

After great disasters and victories, the Allies and democracy won. There are many books written about the huge battles and leaders who determined the outcome and secured this victory, and certainly, there are many more to come. That's how it should be. On the other hand, there are aspects of the war that are not so well-known, so they deserve more of our attention. One of those aspects is the stories of the women who actively participated in the war as agents and spies, helping and guiding the resistance against the Nazis in occupied territories and cooperating with the Allied armies to facilitate their fights against the Nazi forces.

# Chapter 1:

# Breaking Boundaries—Women's

# Impact in WWII

Although women's role as spies and agents in World War II is not an unknown or hidden issue, it certainly deserves more attention and documentation. That doesn't mean women who participated in and had an impact on the war are not remembered and honored, and we will acknowledge some of them in this book. The Second World War has been the primary subject captivating anyone with an interest in modern history. The point of this book is to provide a more complete view of WWII.

To participate in war, it was considered that you had to be strong, courageous, and heroic—which up to this point was usually thought to be the qualities of men. Women were thought to be gentle, peaceful, empathetic, weak, and sensitive. We now know this perspective underestimated women's ability and capacity to be warriors.

This book is based on genuine history, proving that many traditional assumptions are groundless and counterproductive. War is not a male or female activity but a phenomenon that involves societies as a whole. No one is immune to its consequences, and no one can neglect to offer their best in the collective war effort.

The previously held views don't belong to societies that must fight for their existence. While these lines are being written, two bloody wars are unfolding in areas very close to the West, and the illusions of eternal peace of the previous historical period give way to more realistic views of the modern world and what we should expect or be prepared for.

Moreover, in both these wars, we can see that women are as equally involved as men in the broader war effort. Their impact on the ideals, political, ethical, administrative, and diplomatic levels, and sometimes even on the battlefield, is crucial and no less important than that of men. Actually, nobody cares about this kind of distinction when the population fights for survival.

We hope our societies won't experience this ultimate test again. History can teach us all we need to know without direct experience. The focus of this book begins with an overview of women spies and agent's roles in this chapter before we go on with our nine ladies' stories.

# Rosie the Riveter

The Second World War brought and accelerated significant changes in women's roles, creating new opportunities and responsibilities. As the war continued to grow, so did the needs and the demands of the war efforts. With millions of men on the fronts or at least conscripted by the military, the advanced industries of the 20th century had to be filled with female workers in order to continue their production. A great part of this production was of military necessity, as weapons, aircraft, equipment, munition, and many other supplies were needed by the combatting armies.

This created a massive difference from previous historical eras, where the modern industry was much smaller or non-existent. In earlier times, wars didn't have the capacity to transform society as obviously or immediately as the one we are talking about. However, by the late 1930s, industrialized countries demanded a massive presence of industrial workers. With the circumstances of the war and the massive conscription of men, those workers had to be women. That simple fact resulted in huge numbers of women leaving their homes to work in big factories and socialize in a way they hadn't done before. This is when the iconic symbol of Rosie the Riveter came to life, epitomizing all those women who worked hard with enthusiastic determination for the military industries and the industries of wartime.

Industrial production played a pivotal role in the collective war effort, as the powerful American industry produced an enormous amount of materials that provided all the firepower the Allied armies needed to be effective and eventually victorious on the battlefields, helping to aid the British and even the Soviet efforts after the German invasion of the Soviet Union. The women welders, riveters, and assembly line workers were crucial to industrial production, and their entering the factories transformed the perception of women's role in society in general, which, until then, related more to staying at home. That process began as the Industrial Revolution grew in the 19th century. Still, World War II had an essential impact on accelerating that particular transformation of society.

# Women in the Military

With women now having a large presence and impact on industrial production, WWII pushed societies to involve women in actual military professions and activities. We already said that war had always been something that involved society as a whole and that women had always had an important role in it. However, the massive demands for more personnel for the WWII effort brought unprecedented numbers of women directly into military service. Firstly, nurses, who often were close to the front lines and provided crucial medical care to wounded soldiers, saving lives and helping with a series of functions and services, such as evacuation units, transports, and transfers, and of course, working in larger hospitals away from the battlefields.

Many countries' military units had a high percentage of women in the ranks of their auxiliary units. The United States established women's corps in all three basic branches: the army, the navy, and the air force. Even though public opinion was mostly against women entering into the armed forces, the necessities of the war and the simple objective that the military needed more people opened the doors to female personnel. For the US Army, the Women's Army Auxiliary Corps (WAAC) unit was created on May 15, 1942. The WAAC had initially followed the model of the British women's military units after Army Chief of Staff George C. Marshall was interested in them and thought that they could be helpful to the US Army, too. He was proved right by the WAAC's efficiency, and they definitely overcame any objections to the use of women by the armed forces.

It all began with 800 women who joined the unit in the spring of 1942. They were divided into three contingents after test results that determined their abilities, and they got basic training as switchboard operators, mechanics, and bakers. During the following months and years, many more women joined the army, and their areas of expertise grew as contingents of stenographers, drivers, postal clerks, and clerk-typists were established. On July 1, 1943, the WAAC became the Women's Army Corps (WAC) as it went from an auxiliary unit to an active combat unit. When the unit was transformed from auxiliary to active, it introduced a physical training manual. Women who joined the army needed to have the best physical condition, as the aim of the training was to make them capable of replacing men in combat if necessary, and in general, being able to accomplish every mission their leaders would assign them. Until the end of the war, a total of around 150,000 women had served in the WAAC and WAC, offering precious services to the US armed forces and contributing to the Allies' victory. The official insignia of the Women's Army Corps was the head of the ancient Greek goddess Athena with her helmet.

In the US Navy, the women's unit was founded in July 1942 under the name United States Naval Reserve (Women's Reserve). It became known as—and is still called—and is still called—WAVES, which came from Women Accepted for Volunteer Emergency Service. In the case of the Navy, there was an even more specific reason to reinforce its ranks: the Japanese attack at Pearl Harbor on December 7, 1941. Since that day, it was clear that the United States would enter the war on both fronts, against Germany and Italy in Europe and Africa and against Japan in East Asia-Pacific. The latter meant that massive naval battles were underway against the powerful imperial Japanese navy. American women had to step up as well. At the same time, many in Congress and the Navy itself had to overcome their initially unfavorable opinions toward women in uniforms. Indeed, the US Congress voted to establish the WAVES on July 21, 1942, and on July 30, President Franklin D. Roosevelt signed the law. His wife, Eleanor, and Navy's Women's Advisory Council, Margaret Chung, had played an essential role in promoting the idea. Thousands of women served in the WAVES, which reached 86,291 members at their maximum force. They served at 900 stations, doing many different jobs, from medicine and various office services to engineering and parachute riggers.

For their part, the US Air Force created the Women's Flying Training Detachment and the Women's Auxiliary Ferrying Squadron in September 1942. Then, on August 5, 1943, they folded the two organizations to establish the Women Airforce Service Pilots (WASP). The tasks of WASP allowed more male pilots to become available for combat. The female pilots covered a series of functions like testing aircraft, training new pilots, and transferring airplanes. The WASP members were not officers of the Airforce but civilian employees of the Airforce, and they were not involved in actual combat.

Nevertheless, their contribution was very important, as around 900 male pilots were able to enter combat squadrons thanks to the female pilots' activity. They made around 80% of the aircraft transfers during the war, delivering 12,652 airplanes. Those were women dedicated to helping their country's war effort and also to flying since entering the WASP was also extremely difficult, as we can see from the statistics: more than 25,000 women applied, but only 1,830 began the training, and only 1,074 completed it (U.S. Department of Defense, 2016).

# Women Spies and Agents

There have always been female spies and agents in history, such as the famous Mata Hari during World War I. We can suppose, though, having read the above paragraphs, that their impact and numbers in World War II were even greater, following the broader war-related female activity we've seen. The use of more female spies during WWII was due to strategic considerations and operational needs, namely the necessity for as many people as possible to be on various fronts and behind enemy lines.

All the involved countries soon understood there was a need for agents capable of infiltrating enemy territories and gathering information, as well as sabotaging operations of the enemy army and infrastructure.

Political and military leaders began using female agents, initially thinking that they had some qualities that could make them very helpful to the intelligence agencies' operations. Those qualities were their perceived ability to act in more discrete and subtle ways than men, to pass unnoticed and not raise suspicions. Moreover, women often have high communication skills and can relate easily with other people, which could help them to collect information through light social interactions and casual small talk. Another factor in favor of women being activated as agents and spies was their richer wardrobe and the possibility to change hairstyles, face, and body appearance more easily and with great variety.

As we shall see in the following chapters, female agents operated in several roles. Mostly, they were couriers but also wireless operators, creators and organizers of agents and spies' networks, and collaborators of local resistance groups. There were also cases of female spies who had the capacity and connection to access sensitive information and gather intelligence. Women agents and spies operated, risked, and often died just like their male counterparts. There were no exceptions or special treatment for those who chose to contribute to their countries' war efforts.

A very important aspect we must remember is all those women were volunteers, as there wasn't any military conscription for women like there is now in a few countries. Those women joined the military or agencies and services related to the war on a voluntary basis, moved by a sense of responsibility and the will to offer any help they could give to their countries in that extremely difficult moment. Especially those who chose to become agents and spies had to often put themselves in the dangerous situations behind enemy lines and inside enemy-occupied territories. There wasn't any other incentive than fighting for freedom against Nazism.

This meant that they often had only the minimum training before they were sent on missions, given the urgent necessity of the war. There have been controversies about some of the choices the intelligence agencies made, in cases of young women who had mixed reports from their trainers, and at least some would say they were underqualified. There were doubts about their ability to accomplish their missions in the extremely harsh conditions of the war. Sometimes, the decisive criteria may not have been operational readiness but other qualities, like linguistic abilities, cultural backgrounds, familiarity with a country, character traits, or just an emergency and the need to send people to the battlegrounds as soon as possible.

Nevertheless, intense physical training was absolutely necessary, and the female agents had to pass through that to develop endurance and stamina, like their male colleagues. When you have to penetrate areas controlled by the Nazis and full of German roadblocks, enter a gunfight, or if the Nazis are coming after you, it doesn't matter if you are a man or a woman. You have to be able to do whatever it takes to survive and accomplish your mission. It may be shooting, hand-to-hand combat, climbing, running, or keeping your cool while you face mortal danger, and the most minor mistake can give you away. Female agents had to be ready for all that, and the training was not that easy.

Last but not the least was the possibility of getting arrested. Agents had to be prepared physically, mentally, and psychologically in case they were captured. Protecting their team and keeping their organization and its operations and plans safe and secret could be their last and most important contribution. The interrogation simulation was often the most brutal and the hardest point of the whole training.

Resilience and mental toughness, adaptability, and communication with people from other countries in different cultural environments were as important as physical strength and stamina and the use of arms. Also, an agent had to have some knowledge of the basic aspects of strategy: the strategic plans of their political and military leaders, the movements of their armies, the situation on the fronts, and what the enemy was doing or trying to do. The body, the psychology, and the mind must all be ready for the tasks ahead, as war is a situation that requires complete focus and commitment. This was achieved through specialized training schools that the women attended.

In general terms, female agents and spies demonstrated they were effective and efficient beyond all expectations. Their impact in secret operations complemented those of the military and industrial production, bringing a much larger integration of women in roles previously much more strictly associated with men. World War II created necessities in a wide range of fields and functioned also as a catalyst for a transformation in society that brought women much closer to politics and the military than before.

# Chapter 2:

# Nancy Wake—The White Mouse of WWII

*I learned that courage was not the absence of fear but triumph over it.* –Nelson Mandela

Nancy Grace Augusta Wake would become a member of the French Resistance and then of the Special Operations Executive (SOE) during World War II. However, her early life had nothing to do with the military or intelligence services and nothing to do with France and Europe, making her story more intriguing.

# Escaping a Troubled Childhood

Nancy Wake was born in Roseneath, Wellington, New Zealand, on August 30, 1912, the sixth child of Charles Augustus Wake and Ella Rosieur Wake. Her childhood was not emotionally happy. She had a very close and warm relationship with her father, but when he went to the United States to work on making a movie about Maori culture, he abandoned the family and never returned. This left Nancy with her mother, who never showed Nancy affection or love. Once, she found a paper with an inappropriate rhyme taught to Nancy by her dear friend Jenny. As she had a strict Christian faith, the mother dragged Nancy to her school by her ear, demanding she be punished. The teacher was furious and began punishing her. Nancy was afraid, and trying to escape punishment, mentioned her friend, who was then punished, too.

Writing about her life, Nancy indicated that those three hurtful experiences were very important and taught her a lot. First, the betrayal of her father made her understand she should be extremely careful of whom she trusted. Second, the bad relationship and lack of affection from her mother prompted her to become independent and self-sufficient. Third, seeing her friend punished because of her made Nancy swear that she would never ever betray a person close to her again. Those painful lessons would help her a great deal in her war activities.

Nancy left her home to live alone when she was only 16 years old, working for two years as a nurse. But then, something unexpected happened. After her parents had failed her, her aunt left her enough money for her to travel to some of the great cities of the modern world. Nancy went to New York, London, and Paris and loved the French capital so much that she decided to stay there.

In Paris, Nancy met and fell in love with Henri Fiocca, a wealthy French industrialist, and she married him on November 30, 1939, while she worked as a journalist. She had a happy marriage. When she traveled to Vienna as a journalist, she saw the Nazis abuse the Jews. It made her hate the Nazis deeply, promising herself that if she had the opportunity, she would do anything to stop the horrors of Nazism, even if it put her safety and fulfilling life at risk.

## A Parisian Lady Becomes a Resistance Fighter

In June 1940, the Wehrmacht successfully completed its stunning *blitzkrieg* against the French Army, leaving the French government with no option other than to sign an armistice and accept defeat. Paris and Northern France became part of Adolf Hitler's Third Reich, while a German-controlled French government would govern the rest of the country, known as the Vichy France. We'll talk about that more in the following chapter. That was a disaster for the French people, but also the opportunity for Nancy to actively oppose the Nazis and their plans of dominating Europe.

During the summer of 1940, the French Resistance began almost immediately after the fall of France. At the same time, the Royal Air Force was fighting against the Luftwaffe in the air of Manić, Serbia, throwing the first blows of the war on German soil, and on July 16, British Prime Minister Winston Churchill funded the SOE. As he said, SOE's purpose would be to "set Europe ablaze," "counteract German brutality by means of sabotage and subversion," and deliberately collaborate with the French Resistance.

When Nancy Wake was living as a typical wealthy Parisien lady during the 1930s, nobody could have ever imagined her future role. However, her financial and social status made it easier for her to join the resistance at the beginning of the German occupation. Obviously, it was hard for the Germans to imagine that a wealthy woman would risk her safety and stability to embrace an activity that could lead to death or prison. At the same time, that perception was a great advantage for those who chose to risk everything, such as Nancy, who by that time lived in Marseille, in Vichy France.

Nancy obtained false papers so she could hide her true identity and also asked her husband to buy an ambulance. Her idea was initially to help Allied soldiers, aviators who had been shot down, Jews, and resistance members to leave for safe places. Captain Ian Garrow created the resistance network she was a member of, which was later called the Pat O'Leary Line. Over time, Nancy became more involved, using her financial capacity to free captured members of the resistance by bribing guards of the prisons.

Things became harder when the German forces occupied Vichy France in November 1942, while the war in North Africa was ranging, and the Allies had made serious progress on that front; again, we'll talk more about it in the following chapter. Nancy's role had become increasingly more important, bringing her to the point of being a suspect for the *Gestapo*. The official German secret police began following and watching her, and by 1943, Nancy had the unlikely honor of being rated as no. 1 on the German agents' "most wanted" list. The Gestapo also offered a price of five million francs to those who would help capture her.

Nancy had always managed to escape and go on with the resistance, using her many different false identities and other, more charming methods. As she later said: "I'd see a German officer on the train or somewhere, sometimes dressed in civvies, but you could pick 'em. So, instead of raising suspicions I'd flirt with them, ask for a light and say my lighter was out of fuel... A little powder and a little drink on the way, and I'd pass their posts and wink and say, 'Do you want to search me?' God, what a flirtatious little bastard I was." (Leech, 2011).

Nancy's great ability to pass through controls and escape had also earned her the nickname the "White Mouse." However, by 1943, the situation escalated as the network had been compromised, so it was too risky to stay in France. So, Nancy finally decided to leave the country and pass to Britain through the Pyrenees, which would prove to be a much harsher and more dangerous adventure than she had hoped. Leaving her husband behind was incredibly difficult but her journey to the safety of Britain was actually much harder. She had to try six times before finally making it. During those attempts, she had to live cinema-like scenes, such as being shot, staying for days without having anything to eat, getting close to dying in the cold, spending nights in a sheep pen, and, of course, the usual scene of jumping from a moving train. But this was not a movie, this was her life!

During those adventures, she was momentarily arrested in Toulouse for four days. Albert Guérisse, the leader of the Pat O'Leary Line, helped her escape by coming up with a crazy story about Nancy being his mistress and trying to hide her cheating from her husband.

When Nancy finally made it to Great Britain, she was immediately recruited by the British SOE, whose officials already knew everything about her. They put her in the French section of the SOE, the F Section, which had another 38 women. At the end of the war, Nancy would be one of the 27 women that survived of those 39. The section's leader was Maurice Buckmaster, and their work would be even more active and explosive than the one Nancy had in France. Literally explosive. In the SOE, Nancy got explosives and guerilla training, becoming a saboteur. Their job was to sabotage the Nazis in the occupied territories, collaborating with local resistance. Nancy's abilities were astonishing, as were her flashing eyes and strength of character. She impressed the SOE trainers with her vitality, her fast and accurate shooting, and fieldcraft.

Nancy's mission was to help the Maquis, the small local groups of the French Resistance, who were often spontaneous and untrained. She would make sure they had all the necessary provisions, and she would offer them leadership and training in becoming really dangerous to the Germans. She returned to France in a way she would never have anticipated: jumping out of a military airplane with a parachute and a bag full of money and plans. Once she landed on April 30, 1944, in the Auvergne, she found her partners with whom she would be working, SOE colleague John Farmer, and Henri Tardivat, a French member of the resistance. Soon after, a wireless operator also joined the team, which was crucial in order to be in contact with SOE's central office in London to organize parachute drops in France to reinforce the resistance with explosives and weapons. The name of the wireless operator was Denis Rake, while the code name used by Nancy in this mission was Helene. The head of the maquis in the region was Émile

Coulaudon, who initially was not very cooperative with the British. He was told he should trust them and work with them by General Charle de Gaulle who French Forces of the Interior organization coordinated the various resistance groups.

So, the force Nancy and her partners had at their disposal was more than 7,000 guerilla fighters. The problem was they weren't a trained unit, and they weren't capable of using the new types of weapons. So, as Nancy later stated the task was to turn this courageous rabble with guns and no organization into a disciplined fighting force.

## Supporting Operation Overlord

The training went on for months, and Nancy's men began engaging in gun battles with the German troops in northern Auvergne while D-Day was approaching. The problem was they became too confident, and Coulaudon wanted to prove that they could liberate areas by themselves without the Allied armies reaching the region first. However, that was far from the truth. In late May and early June 1944, they suffered some heavy blows by the Germans.

On June 6, 1944, when Operation Overlord started, Nancy's Maquis were ready! They had targets and some designated strategic points to blow up making it difficult for the Germans to keep moving, and hopefully, stopping them altogether. On D-Day, they had great success in blowing up their targets. Nancy was a little disappointed because she had missed all the action. Farmer had led the operation, while she had collected a weapons instructor who arrived that day by parachute and brought him to the camp. Bad timing for her!

Nancy soon forgot about her D-Day disappointment as in the following days, her Maquis group had a great deal to do, and they did it really well—blowing up bridges, railways, roads, and anything to hamper the German movements. The formidable Wehrmacht Hermann Goring's Division was operating in their sector. Their role was to harass and create obstacles to the German advances helping the Allies win the greater battle waging in Normandy.

Four days after the beginning of Operation Overlord, Nancy's mission became even harder. The Germans had taken notice of her Maquis division and launched more intense attacks against them with sizeable forces consisting of 22,000 soldiers. This made the wireless operator Rake hide his wireless set and burn his codes, fearing that he could soon end up in the hands of the Germans. This was bad news for Nancy and the group, as they could no longer communicate with London. Nancy stepped up and said that she was going to solve the problem by contacting another wireless operator in Northern France, who would message London asking them to send a new wireless and codes by parachute to their camp. She would go on a bicycle to the nearest operator who was at Chateauroux, approximately 200 km or more from their camp.

Some of the other leaders of the group thought the plan was too risky. How could she physically travel more than 400 km on a bicycle? How would she avoid the German control points, as they were constantly looking for members of the resistance? All those risks with no one to defend her Nevertheless, in the end, everybody became convinced that she was the best choice for the job because she was the only woman in the group. A woman could flirt with the German soldiers if she came upon a control point, and hopefully, they would let her continue. She had a better chance to pass unnoticed. Who would think a delicate young lady was a Resistance leader in that hellish war? The Germans would be looking for guys like all the others in the group, who would have almost no chance to travel that far.

Nancy covered the distance in a day and a half, and she managed to find a wireless operator. Then, they contacted London and arranged for a new wireless set to be sent the location of her camp. The mission was accomplished, but she still had to return, and because she was already very tired, it would be even harder. Nancy was back in a day and a half and really proud of her accomplishment. This bicycle trip during the Battle of Normandy was so important and difficult to do that Nancy later said that of all her war achievements, it was the one accomplishment that made her most proud.

Some of Nancy's most impressive accomplishments were made following the bicycle mission. She personally led a raid against Montlucon Gestapo's headquarters, killed a sentry with her hands during a raid on a German gun factory so he could not alert the guard, killed a female German spy, and shot to pass through roadblocks. If you can't do these sorts of things, you don't become a leader of the Resistance against the Nazis during WWII. Tardivat, Nancy's French partner during the Normandy mission, said that she was the most feminine woman he had ever met, but when she was fighting, she was more like five men.

# After the War

Despite the Allied victory, the end of the war brought sadness to Nancy. She returned home to find that her husband had been arrested by the Gestapo and killed after being tortured when the Pat Line had been compromised in 1942. Nancy felt awful and thought it was her fault. Her husband would have had nothing to do with the war and the Gestapo if it wasn't for her. She regretted his death for the rest of her life, blaming herself for what had happened. Fortunately, she found happiness again in 1957, when she married John Forward, an officer of the Royal Air Force.

Before that, she was also a candidate for the seat of Barton in Sydney in the 1949 and 1951 Australian elections. Then, she went back to Britain and worked in the department of the Assistant Chief of the Air Staff. In the 1960s, she returned to Australia with her husband, and she became active in politics again. Although she was never elected, she received a huge number of votes in spite of running against very well-established politicians. After her husband died in 1997, she returned to London and became a resident at the Stafford Hotel in St. James' Place, where the Allied troops used to hang out during WWII.

Nancy lived a full life, dying at 98 on August 7, 2011, in London. For her precious service to the Allies against Nazism, she was awarded nine medals. Among them, the George Medal from Britain, the Chevalier de la Légion d'Honneur, the *Croix de Guerre,* and the *Medaille de la Resistance* from France, the Medal of Freedom with Palm from America, and the Companion of the Order of Australia.

# Chapter 3:

# Virginia Hall—The Limping Lady

# of the Resistance

*You never know how strong you are until being strong is your only choice.* –Bob Marley

Virginia Hall was a British Special Operations Executive (SOE) member during WWII, like Nancy Wake, and she also worked with the American Office of Strategic Services (OSS) in France. Just like Nancy in the previous chapter, Virginia also became famous for her war activities in Europe even though she knew nothing of the military before the war and was from another continent.

# Higher Education

Virginia Hall Goillot was born in Baltimore, Maryland, on April 6, 1906. Her parents were Edwin Lee Hall and Barbara Virginia. Young Virginia was highly educated, attending Radcliffe College of Harvard University, Barbara College of Columbia University, and George Washington University after she graduated from Toland Park Country School. She studied economics, and her level of education was exceptional, especially for a woman. Added to this was the fact that as an American, Virginia had studied and learned three foreign languages: German, French, and Italian. In other words, the languages of the three greatest powers of continental Europe, the future principal characters of World War II.

Virginia was apparently an adventurous spirit and a great learner. Not only was she passionate enough to complete all that study, but she also traveled a lot in Europe, where she finished her studies. She traveled and studied in France, Germany, and Austria and worked for a few months in the United States Embassy in Warsaw, Poland, as a Consular Service clerk. But Europe wasn't enough for her. In 1931, Virginia landed in Asia Minor, Turkey, and she went to live in Smyrna (called Izmir by the Turks).

Virginia's stay in Turkey didn't end well. She almost died and had to have her leg amputated below the knee. The story is that Virginia went to hunt some birds, and after tripping on a fence, she accidentally shot her left foot. The situation deteriorated quickly, the wound causing gangrene, putting her life in severe and immediate danger. In the end, the doctors replaced her leg with a wooden appendage. Given the dramatic situation she survived, Virginia felt lucky. Maybe that's why she called her appendage "Cuthbert," expressing her gratitude.

After that awful near-death experience, Virginia went to Venice, Italy, and then Tallinn, Estonia, working as a consular clerk. Later, she returned to the United States and worked at the State Department as a consular clerk. She sincerely wanted to do more and she tried several times to enter the diplomatic agency of the U.S. but was unsuccessful. One of the reasons probably was a rule existing at the time that people with disabilities shouldn't become diplomats.

# Ending Up in the Middle of a War and Becoming an Agent

Virginia had had enough by March 1939. She resigned from her job as a consular clerk at the State Department and did what she loved to do: moving to another country. This time, she went to France, and in February 1940, she was in the unusual position of working as an ambulance driver for the French army. This is where the German invasion and the fall of France found her, in May and June 1940. After that, she moved again, this time to Spain. Here, she happened to meet George Bellows, who was an officer of British intelligence, who thought that Virginia could be an excellent operative. He gave her the number of Nicolas Bodington, an agent of the SOE, to find her a job in England. So, after living through the frustration of not becoming a diplomat, Virginia would have the opportunity to be part of an organization that dynamically influenced World War II.

Virginia Hall did the SOE training from April to August 1941, and on August 23, she was in Vichy, France, under the cover of being a reporter for the New York Post. Vichy France was the minimally independent state created by the Germans in the southern regions of France, with the capital at Vichy. It was led by Marshal Philippe Pétain, the World War I French national hero, who sadly agreed to become a traitor at 84 years old and was convicted of treason after WWII. At the same time, Paris and the northern part of France, as well as a strip in the western part, were occupied and incorporated into the German empire. The Germans controlled Vichy France, yet it was somewhat more accessible for a spy to settle and work there instead of inside the Third Reich's official territories. Hall, who presented herself as a reporter, had the opportunity to interview a lot of people and gather useful information and details that could be used for military purposes. People like Virginia who are behind enemy lines and inside enemy territory are the eyes and ears of military planners. When they manage to provide accurate information, it becomes very important for military preparations and operations.

Virginia's job was to arrange contacts, supervise the distribution of wireless sets, find places where her partner agents could hide, and find people they could bribe to obtain information. She was the second woman to be sent to France during World War II by the SOE, and her job was crucial. She was the first SOE female agent to stay for a long period in France, as she founded a circuit of agents. One of her recruits was Germaine Guerin, who owned a luxury brothel in Lyon, where Virginia had settled. Guerin provided several safe places to Virginia and the other SOE agents, and through his employees, who were sex workers, he was able to pass pieces of information to Virginia and the SOE because German officers often visited his brothel.

Virginia also had the responsibility to take care of British aviators who had crashed or been shot down and return them to Britain. If the aviators arrived at Lyon, they could come in contact with her through the American Consulate. The password they were told to use was "I'm a friend of Olivier." Then the Consulate brought them to Virginia, who gave them shelter in Guérin's safehouses, and arranged their transfer to Spain, which was neutral in the conflict even though they were an ally of Hitler and Mussolini, and on to Britain. Dozens of aviators returned home thanks to this system and Virginia's effort during the war.

In October 1941, SOE agents arranged a meeting in Marseille to discuss the situation and plan their next moves. Virginia thought it would be risky and dropped the meeting, staying out of danger. Sadly, she was proven right. The French police came to know about the meeting, and they stormed into the place, raiding and arresting twelve SOE agents. Virginia would be very meticulous on security matters in the future. On another occasion, she refused to have contact with an SOE agent who was sent to Lyon because she thought he acted in an amateur way and wasn't attentive to security. She also avoided introducing him to her contacts. Later, the SOE central appointed that agent, Georges Duboudin, to be her supervisor, but she reacted by telling headquarters to lay off. Furthermore, Virginia had minimal contact and worked less with a leader of the French Resistance,

Philippe de Vomécourt, who was perfectly loyal and trustworthy, but again, she thought he wasn't attentive enough in security matters.

# Risky Operations

In the summer of 1942, Georges Bégué, one of the SOE agents who had been arrested in Marseille the previous October, managed to pass letters to Virginia, who then knew that the arrested agents were at Mauzac prison near Bergerac. Then, she organized an elaborate escape plan, recruiting Gaby Block, the wife of one of the agents, Jean-Pierre Block. The plan was that when Gaby was visiting her husband in prison, she would take not only food but also materials that could help him create a pass key to the barracks door. That material was tins of sardines. For her part, Virginia prepared the escape by recruiting people who could help with various tasks, including enabling vehicles for transport and safehouses for the agents to hide in after the escape. One of the people who helped was a priest, who passed a radio inside the prison, and Bégué contacted London from there.

Finally, the escape took place on July 15, 1942, and after high adventure, they managed to evade the French police who were hunting for them and gather on August 11 in Lyon. From there, Virginia's infrastructure and contacts helped them travel to Spain and finally return to England safely. They used the same path Virginia had followed a couple of years earlier. The jailbreak operation was hugely successful because it didn't just save the agents' lives but many of them later returned to France and worked on creating and expanding SOE circuits, using their experience.

The Gestapo reacted to the debacle of their Vichy French allies by sending in 500 Gestapo agents. Their mission was to find the British and French SOE agents and destroy their networks. What happened in the Mauzac prison was a wake-up call for *Abwehr*, the German military intelligence service, and they began operating with much greater consistency in Vichy France. The Germans having had enough of the French Resistance and the SOE. They wanted to eradicate them, as the war was raging on in a massive and unbelievably bloody fashion on the Eastern and North African fronts during 1942.

Even Virginia, who was so scrupulous with safety could be caught off guard. An Abwehr agent, Robert Alesch, who was also a Catholic priest, infiltrated a Paris-based French Resistance network called *Gloria*, and the network's leaders were arrested. The problem for Virginia was that she was in contact with Gloria in May 1942, agreeing to send messages from them to the SOE's headquarters. Alesch, having infiltrated Gloria, contacted Virginia and convinced her he could provide important information. In this way, the Catholic priest infiltrated Virginia's contacts as well in August, causing damage to her network and confusing SOE headquarters. Some wireless operators were arrested thanks to his operation. He sent misleading reports and messages to London, which appeared to be sent by Virginia herself.

That was the world of secret agents during World War II. Furthermore, the German retaliation was far from complete, as the unfolding of the broader war on the fronts created more urgent conditions for everybody. The turning points of the war were approaching, but all was just chaos, pressure, blood, and effort.

In July, the first Battle of El Alamein, 150 miles west of Cairo, Egypt, had no clear winner and ended in a stalemate. On October 23, the battle restarted more intensely. Two weeks later, the British Eighth Army and French, Greek, and Libyan allies, under Field Marshal Bernard Law Montgomery, "Monty," had decisively pushed back the German Afrika Korps and the Italian forces of the Axis under Field Marshal Ervin Rommel, one of the most charismatic figures of the war. Virginia was informed by the American consulate in Lyon on November 7, American and more British forces were heading to North Africa. They would land in Algeria and Morocco the next day, called Operation Torch. The Axis troops' situation was becoming desperate in North Africa, and their withdrawal from the region was just a matter of time. Hitler responded by occupying Vichy France, ending its nominal independence.

That was bad news for Virginia and the French Resistance, as they would now have to deal with harsher and more direct German suppression without the space they had under the previous regime.

Virginia decided to leave immediately before the occupation was complete; perhaps she knew it was time to flee France after what had happened in the summer, as the danger was now extremely high. So, she left without informing her contacts, first taking the train to Perpignan from Lyon and then covering a distance of 50 miles in two days as she walked her way to Spain through the Pyrenees with the help of a guide.

There is no doubt that the operation was even more difficult due to her wooden leg, "Cuthbert." However, there is a funny story for us: Virginia informed the SOE headquarters that she was about to leave, and she hoped "Cuthbert" wouldn't give her too much trouble on the way; the SOE operators didn't know or didn't recall who "Cuthbert" was, and they responded her that if he was troublesome, she should eliminate him.

Virginia made it to Spain, but that wasn't the end of her difficult trip. She was arrested because she had crossed the border illegally, and she was released only after the American Embassy intervened and convinced the Spanish authorities to let her go. In the following months, Virginia continued to operate for the SOE in Madrid. Then, in July 1943, she returned to London. It didn't take her long to ask the SOE leadership to send her back to France. However, they refused, saying that it would be way too dangerous as she was compromised by their previous operations there. Yet, Virginia Hall wouldn't quit if she had really decided she wanted to do something. So, she took a wireless operator course and requested a job for the Office of Strategic Services (OSS) instead. If the British wouldn't let her return to France, she would do it by working with the Americans. She wanted to return to France so badly that she accepted the job offered her by the OSS, with just the salary of a second lieutenant.

# Back to France

On March 21, Virginia was back in France, at Beg-an-Fry, Britanny. Her cover name on her fake ID was Marcelle Montagne, and her codename for the mission was Diane. She carried with her 500,000 francs. Because of her wooden leg, she couldn't parachute in like Nancy Wake did in the same year, as we saw in the previous chapter. Instead, Virginia arrived in France, traveling on a motor gunboat.

Virginia's second mission in France would be different from the first. Now, it was not about information but about brutal warfare, as the decisive moment in 1944 was approaching after years of bloodshed and destruction. The job for Virginia and her OSS partners was, just like Nancy Wake's, to organize and send materials to the Maquis, the fighters of the French Resistance. D-Day was coming, and the Maquis' role would be to sabotage, launch raids against infrastructure or German soldiers, and do whatever they could to confuse and distract the Germans, allowing the main Allied army to advance on the basic front.

Apart from providing Resistance groups with arms, Virginia had various other activities, mostly south of Paris, like organizing safe houses and creating drop zones. She also attempted to rescue three Resistance members who were prisoners of the Germans but sadly, she didn't succeed in this. That must have been disappointing, as she called those men her "nephews." To avoid suspicion and being captured, Virginia sometimes dressed up like an older milkmaid with filed-down teeth. Apparently, she was so convincing with her grey hair and other traits of a peasant, that she passed unnoticed, and one time, she even sold cheese made by herself to German soldiers. Knowing that if she talked too much, her accent would reveal she was not French, she had always had a French woman with her whom she recruited to do the talking.

Virginia's activity in France also continued during and after the Allied invasion in Normandy on June 6, and she was sent to continue with the Maquis arming and guiding in the south as the American and British forces pushed the Germans back. On August 15, the Allies launched Operation Dragoon, that is, the attack against German forces in southern France, having liberated the north.

Virginia was sent to Haute-Loire one month earlier, and she established her base at Le Chambon-sur-Lignon. The three Maquis battalions she worked with were part of the newly established French Forces of the Interior, and they had a successful impact on the conflict. They conducted several sabotage operations, and they made the German troops at Le Puy-en-Velay withdraw. Yet, things were not idyllic there for Virginia, as the self-proclaimed colonels did not recognize her authority, as officially, she had the low rank of a second lieutenant, and obviously, she was a woman (although she was back to normal, abandoning the old lady disguise). Virginia complained to OSS central that they didn't assure her authority with the people they sent her to work with. The problem was solved in late July after she received enough money and supplies to make everybody happier.

The mission in France was a perfect success by autumn, 1944. Virginia then went to Austria with the OSS member Paul Goillot to work with resistance groups that opposed the Nazis there, too. They returned to France in April 1945 while the war in Europe was coming to an end, with the Allied victory and the Nazis final collapse. Virginia resigned from the OSS after writing reports mentioning people who deserved commendations because of the help they had provided. Her interest in the people she had worked with in those turbulent times in France continued. She went back to Lyon, and there, she learned about every member of the SOE she could.

# After the War

Virginia was hired by the CIA in 1947, breaking boundaries since she was one of the first female employees of the agency. Her job in the CIA was to gather and analyze information related to the activities and influence of the Soviets in European countries. Yet, although her superiors, who knew her work and abilities, supported her, she faced discrimination and lost promotions and positions.

In the 1950s, using her precious expertise, she worked for Operation Gladio, which aimed to set the basis for creating resistance groups in case the Soviets invaded Western Europe. That gave her the opportunity to return and work again in France. She was the first woman to ever be part of this kind of top-secret operation, and she was treated like a living legend.

In 1957, Virginia married Paul Goillot, a former officer of the Office of Strategic Services, with whom she had worked, and they happily settled at a farm in Barnesville, Maryland. She died on July 8, 1982. Virginia Hall was awarded the Distinguished Service Cross of the United States, the Order of the British Empire, and the French *Croix de Guerre*.

# Chapter 4:

# Noor Inayat Khan—The Unsung Heroine

*You gain strength, courage, and confidence by every experience in which you really stop to look fear in the face.* –Eleanor Roosevelt

Often, when historians and biographers mention a person's date and place of birth, that sounds like a mere formality, just the basic information of the person's origins. In the case of Noor Inayat Khan, that important information makes a fascinating story of its own.

# An Atypical Family Background

Noor was born on January 1, 1914, in Moscow, Russia. However, neither of her parents were Russian, as they came from very different countries, cultural backgrounds, and religions. So, what was the story, and how did they come together and in Russia? Her father, Inayat Khan, was an Indian Muslim born in Baroda, Bombay Presidency. Her mother, Pirani Ameena Begum, was an American, born Ora Ray Baker in Albuquerque, New Mexico. The two had met during Noor's father's travels in the United States. He was a musician and a Sufi teacher, living in Europe, and apparently, a wealthy and highly cultured person. Added to that, his family was composed of ancestral nobles and classical musicians from both lineages. The fanciest fact is that his great-grandfather was the sultan of Mysore; his name was Tipu Sultan. Later, Inayat Khan became the leader of the Sufi Order International, which was called the Sufi Order of the West and is now called the Inayati Order.

Somehow, on the first day of 1914, Noor's parents were in Moscow, and that is where she was born. Nevertheless, she was not meant to live in the Russian capital, not even on her first birthday. By the summer of 1914, while World War I, once called simply the Great War, was entering the scene of history, the family decided to leave Russia. They went to London and settled at Bloomsbury. We don't know the precise reasons, but it's compelling to think that baby Noor's parents thought it would be safer, understanding the terrible shape the Tsarist regime and Russia had become by then. That would be a great origin for a future WWII agent of the Special Operations Executive, who was the first female wireless operator the SOE sent to France during the Nazi occupation.

We can't avoid it, so let's say it now: Noor did not survive the war. She died at the Dachau concentration camp on September 13, 1944. She was 30 years old. But she didn't die in vain. Noor is one of the many soldiers and fighters of numerous nations who gave their lives to defeat Nazi tyranny, among many additional civilian victims of that huge bloody war.

Many years before that, and shortly after the previous huge and bloody war had finished, Noor and her family moved again, this time to France, in a town near Paris called Suresnes. They moved into a new house in 1920, which was offered to them by a donor of the Sufi movement, thanks to Inayat Khan's activity as a prominent Sufi teacher. Unfortunately, he died seven years later, when Noor was only 13 years old. So, from a very young age, she had to take care of much more than what a shy and quiet teen girl should have to. Noor had three younger siblings she took responsibility for, as her mother was really devastated by sorrow at her father's premature death.

Nevertheless, Noor did not abandon her desires. In the following years, she studied child psychology at Sorbonne and music at the Paris Conservatory, and she began writing poems and stories for children. She learned to compose music for piano and harp by Nadia Boulanger, and she wrote her children's stories in both French and English, and magazines regularly published them. Noor's children's stories were also played on French radio. Her career as a writer went to the next level when the Second World War was about to explode. In 1939, Londoner publisher George G. Harrap and Co. recognized her talent and published her book *Twenty Jataka Tales*. The original *Jataka tales*, which inspired her to write this book, were a part of the Buddhist tradition, a fact that indicates the extent of Noor's education and personal culture, thanks to her peculiar family history and her interests.

# The Sensitive Pacifist Who Decided to Become a Warrior

But WWII was about to enter the scene, and it did so in a dramatic fashion in France, as we have already seen in the previous chapters. Don't think that Noor just jumped in and became a war heroine. That wasn't the case. Talented young writer and musician Noor left the country with her family while the German troops were occupying it, and they went to England by sea from the port of Bourdeaux on June 22, 1940.

However, soon, something rather unexpected happened. Just a few months later, in November 1940, Noor decided to join the Women's Auxiliary Air Force and to take the training to become a wireless operator. After she finished the training, in June 1941, she was assigned to work at a bomber training school. However, that wasn't enough for Noor, who wanted real action, and, most of all, she wanted to fight against Nazism. The same was true for her brother Vilayat. Indeed, the reasons behind their decision to join the British armed forces and actively enter the war were strictly moral, and maybe surprisingly, political. Noor had a sensitive and dreamy character and pacifist ideals, but she understood that only military force could defeat the Nazis, and additionally, she thought about her father's country. If some Indians could offer a meaningful contribution to the Allied victory in the war and be respected and admired, that would be helpful for India as this could sway public opinion in Britain in favor of Indians, helping them in their independence struggle.

Noor's desire to have a more active role would become a reality in the first months of 1943 when she was assigned to the Air Ministry, Directorate of Air Intelligence, seconded to First Aid Nursing Yeomanry, and later sent for special training to Aylesbury, Buckinghamshire. This time, it was not just about wireless operators as the training specifically focused on wireless operators in occupied territories. Her trainers thought she was fast and accurate, and her previous training certainly gave her an advantage over the other trainees. Moreover, she was the first woman in this role. Before her, the women sent to Aylesbury were trained as couriers, not wireless operators in occupied territories.

The last and most difficult phases of the training were held in Beaulieu. There, Noor and the other trainees had to accomplish a simulation of a real mission. For a wireless operator like her, the mission was to find a post, a safe place in a city, where they could transmit to headquarters, or in this case, the instructors. But there was also a villain in the scenario, an enemy agent who they didn't know was after them, trying to detect them. The training was completed with a horrible Gestapo interrogation, a simulation of a real situation in case the trainees ended up captured by the Germans as agents. Noor was terrified, and according to the reports, she was trembling and had almost lost her voice after the interrogation.

Once the training was concluded, there were doubts about Noor's ability to work in the field. The instructors thought that although she had worked hard and was keen during the training, she lacked ruse, capacity to deceit, and had a very gentle demeanor for a job like that. She seemed childlike and not "overburdened with brains" as the instructor who wrote the final report put it. They thought she was unstable and temperamental, had an extremely feminine character, and was eager to please others and adapt herself to others' moods, giving away information too easily. Above all, she expressed that she didn't want to work in cases in which she would have to be "two-faced." Many of the traits they detected in her would be positive in normal life: kind, emotionally expressive, with great imagination, and aversion to being deceitful. But these qualities could be a drawback if you had to work behind enemy lines in a world war.

The list of the disadvantages mentioned by the instructors went on, including clumsiness, not jumping very well, and fear of weapons. There were some good qualities, too, such as running fast, trying hard to overcome her fear of weapons, and tapping the keys of the wireless set faster each day. Furthermore, Noor was unquestionably committed to the training and the scope of becoming an agent and capable of having a positive impact on the war effort, as the officer for F Section, Vera Atkins, noted.

The newly trained agents stayed in Buckinghamshire for a while after their training to prepare themselves for their missions. However, during that period, things did not seem to go so well for Noor. Her conducting officer said to Atkins that she looked really sad and troubled about what was ahead of her, and two other agents wrote to the officer that Noor should not be sent on a mission. Atkins called her back to London, where they discussed the situation. She told Noor that if she didn't want to go on with that job, which was alright, the only bad thing for the SOE would be for her to fail her partners. Noor denied she was unhappy or had any doubts that she could be a successful agent in France; instead, she claimed to be very confident. Her hesitant attitude in Buckinghamshire was a result of something totally different: her having to leave her always grieving widowed mother. So, they came to an agreement. In case she was missing during the mission, the SOE would not tell her mother unless it was absolutely certain that she was dead. After that conversation, Atkins's final decision was that Noor was ready and could be sent to France as a wireless operator, even though she was not a super agent as her training had been somewhat hasty. Noor was fluent in French, she was technically competent as a wireless operator, and there weren't many experienced and super-capable agents to choose from, anyway. There was also a great urgency to send people to France.

## On a Mission

While Noor was under training, the SOE decided to use the female couriers as wireless operators since they had proven to be successful. That meant they had the most dangerous job an agent could have. The operator's job was to keep their regional network connected to London, transmitting and receiving signals regarding sabotage operations or information about the locations of resistance groups that needed arms. Coordinating resistance operations and groups to produce a cohesive strategy was not achievable without proper communication.

The problem was that, as the war wore on, the operators' susceptibility to detection increased. The times were strict. Everything should be done within 20 minutes, or else the German detection vans could trace the signals and the source of them. The operators had to transmit reports and information really quickly if they wanted to stay relatively safe in enemy territory. But even that was not a guarantee of safety, as detecting the signals was not the only way for the Germans to catch the Allied wireless operators. There was an easier way, and there was nothing the operators could do about it except hope they would be lucky: The Germans could catch them while they were relocating the wireless set to a new location. There were no excuses or cover stories for that. It's easy to understand that the death or capture of a wireless operator was not unusual in those years.

Regardless of the risks and her brother trying to convince her to drop the mission, Noor departed the night of June 16, 1943, and landed in Nazi-occupied France during the early hours of June 17. Her code name for the mission was "Madeleine," and her cover ID was Jean-Marie Regnier. Two other female agents had landed with her that night, Diana Rowden and Cecily Lefort. In every landing, there was a "reception committee," as the SOE called it, in a rather humorous British way, consisting of a group of SOE agents and French allies. Noor's mission would not be to create a new network of agents like Nancy Wake and Virginia Hall. On the contrary, Noor should be the wireless operator for a network that already existed.

Only a week into the mission, serious problems arose for Noor and her partners. On June 24, the Germans had already tightened the grip around her network. The head of the SOE F Section, Colonel Maurice Buckmaster, told Noor she had better return to England immediately, as the situation had turned dangerous. However, Noor insisted on continuing her mission because, at the time, she thought she was the only wireless operator who had remained in Paris. In the end, they agreed that she would remain, but without sending any more messages to London that could be detected by the Germans. Instead, she would only receive signals with instructions and information from the SOE headquarters.

Unfortunately, things got worse for Noor. Someone betrayed her. According to information after the war, the most credible version is the traitor was Renée Garry, who was indeed tried for that after the war and wasn't convicted by only one vote. She was the sister of Emile Garry, who was the leader of a sub-group of Noor's network. The traitor was probably paid 100,000 francs, and her motives could also have been personal She might have been jealous of Noor because she felt the interest and affection of France Antelme, one of their SOE agent partners, had been taken away from her by Noor's arrival.

Noor was captured by the Germans, probably on October 13, 1943. She was transferred to the *Sicherheitsdienst* (SD) headquarters and was interrogated. There, unlike what had happened in the simulation during her training, she remained undaunted. After the war, the chief of SD in Paris at the time, Hans Josef Kieffer, said that Noor didn't give the Germans a clue and instead kept telling lies to mislead them. Moreover, she tried to escape two times from the building at 84 Avenue Foch, Paris, where the German occupiers had established the SD headquarters in France.

Nevertheless, the SD found another way to get information out of Noor. They managed to do that by examining her notebooks, where she had written down all the signals she had sent to SOE headquarters in London as a wireless operator. She had done that, violating the security protocols of the agency, probably because she simply didn't know them well due to her hasty training. That way, the Germans were finally able to send misleading signals to London, making the SOE believe they were coming from Noor. There is an intriguing debate on this because Noor had a particularly heavy-handed style in transmitting Morse messages due to chilblains. That quality gave her the awesome nickname "Bang Away Lulu" in SOE's internal circles. So, one could think that the operators should have understood that something was not right with the fake messages sent by the Germans to create confusion, imitating Noor. On the other hand, German operators were far too competent not to be adept at any possible style. Furthermore, when Sonya Olschanezky, a SOE agent who had been recruited in France, managed to indirectly inform the SOE headquarters that the SD had captured Noor, Buckmaster didn't believe the message because he didn't know anything about Olschanezky and considered it unreliable. We'll discuss this case again in Chapter 7.

The world of secret agents is messy. In that period, Henri Déricourt, who was the F Section officer responsible for the landings and was the head of the "reception committee" the night Noor landed in France, intentionally gave away secrets to the SD. He later justified this by claiming that he was also working for the MI6, the British intelligence agency, without the SOE knowing it. So, in his version, giving away real secrets to the Germans was part of a broader complex plan that aimed to deceive them at a higher level, heading to Operation Overlord of June 1944. The problem was that those intentional treasons aiming to deceive the Germans at higher levels had very real effects at the level at which Noor and her partners were operating. Apparently, they were the main reason the Germans captured three other SOE agents with Noor.

Tragically, another reason for the capture and death of more SOE agents was the fact that the SOE continued to receive the fake German messages from Noor and as a result, unknowingly, provided crucial information back to the Germans. What made this more tragic is the fact that one of the agents executed by the Nazis was Sonya Olschanezky, who had informed SOE headquarters earlier of Noor's arrest, but they hadn't believed her.

# Fighting to the End

Noor managed to escape from the SD headquarters at 84 Avenue Foch on November 25, 1943. She was with SOE agent John Renshaw Starr and a French resistance leader named Léon Faye. They escaped from the roof of the building. However, they didn't get very far, as the Germans came to know about the jailbreak very quickly and reacted immediately, arresting them and bringing them back again. After that, they demanded that she sign a declaration in which she promised she wouldn't attempt to escape again. Noor refused to sign it, and on November 27, the Germans sent her to Germany and put her in prison at Pforzheim. That situation, officially called "safe custody," was awful. Because of her attitude, the Nazis classified Noor as very dangerous. The prisoners remained in isolation, most of the time with chained hands and feet, and that's what happened to Noor for ten straight months. No wonder other prisoners sometimes heard her crying during those months. Nevertheless, she didn't reveal any information and did not cooperate with the Germans.

Maybe for that reason, they transferred her to the Dachau concentration camp on September 12, 1944. Without any kind of trial or further investigation, the very next day, at dawn, they executed her with three other women. Reportedly, Noor was beaten badly by an SS officer and then shot behind the head. We can be sure that her spirit was never broken, though, as even in that terrible condition, right before she died, she fought back against Nazi tyranny by saying "Liberté."

Noor Inayat Khan was posthumously granted the George Cross in 1949 and the *Croix de Guerre* of France. More recently, on November 8, 2012, Anne, Princess Royal, unveiled Noor's bronze bust in Gordon Square Gardens in London. The bust had been made after a public campaign raised £100,000 to fund it.

# Chapter 5:

# Pearl Witherington—"Pauline"

*Never underestimate the power of a woman!* –Archie Andrews

Pearl Witherington, born as Cecile Pearl Witherington Cornioley, was another female agent of the SOE in France during World War II, like the three women we saw in the previous chapters. The most important difference is Pearl was the only woman who became the leader of a SOE network.

# A British French

Pearl was born in Paris on June 24, 1914, but her parents were British. Her father came from a wealthy family, but he had wasted most of his money and was no longer rich when Pearl was growing up. Furthermore, later, she had to negotiate with her father's creditors to save something from his property. Being capable and a British citizen in France, she made it to the British Embassy in Paris and began to work there. However, in May 1940, the Germans invaded France, and the happy days were over, at least for a while. In December 1940, Pearl, her mother, and her three sisters escaped from France, which was dominated by Germany and the Gestapo at that point. For her, everything was even worse because the war separated her from her fiancé, Henri Cornioley, another employee of the British embassy, whom she had met and become engaged to only recently before the German invasion.

After seven months of wandering and adventures that we don't have the details of, Pearl and her family finally arrived in London in July 1941. She soon decided to join the British armed forces in order to fight against the Nazis and especially the German occupation of France. So, she approached the Women's Auxiliary Air Force of the British Air Ministry as a volunteer and began work there. Then, she was charmed by the possibility of having a more active part in the collective war effort and she found joining the Special Operations Executive, our well-known SOE from the previous chapters, to be the best way to achieve that noble goal. The date was June 8, 1943, when Pearl joined the SOE and began her training.

Interestingly, Pearl was distinguished by her ability to use the gun and her accuracy with the target. Yet, her job in France would not be that of a sniper but instead working as an agent for a SOE network. Her abilities were more than suitable for this role. The training was completed around three months later, and on September 22, 1943, Pearl parachuted into France near Tendu, Indre. The leader of her network was Maurice Southgate, and his courier was Jacquelline Nearne. Pearl's initial job in France would also be that of a courier. Her cover job was selling cosmetics, and her code name for the mission was "Marie." Delightedly, Pearl had the opportunity to reunite with her fiancé Henri whom she was separated from by the war more than three years earlier. He had joined the British military in February 1940, and since the German invasion of France, which had happened shortly after the two had become engaged, she hadn't had the chance to meet him. Now that period was over, she was happy to be fighting for the great cause together with the man she loved.

# Fighting for France and Freedom

Their network was called "Stationer," and it was located in central France, covering a broad area that Pearl had to cross in every direction as she was a courier and had to transport messages continuously. This wasn't a comfortable job, seeing as there wasn't a provision for five-star hotels for the couriers, instead, they had to stay and sleep literally anywhere they could. Some occasional safe houses, but then days and nights in trains, in the streets, under bridges, living the nomadic or homeless life of a wanderer. There could also be health issues, and indeed, Pearl suffered from rheumatism for some weeks and had to stop her activity. Another risk for the couriers, and of course, everybody in the SOE or the French Resistance, was being discovered as an agent and captured by the Gestapo or the police of the German-controlled French regime, who had several control points in various posts all over the country. Pearl passed many similar control points and managed to get away with them; apparently, her cover as a cosmetics lady was convincing.

That wasn't the case for the leader of her network, Southgate, whose true identity was discovered, and the Germans arrested him on May 1, 1944, less than a month before D-Day. The Gestapo brought him to the concentration camp at Buchenwald. In that case, Pearl was lucky, as she was with Southgate just before he got captured. She reacted immediately and formed a new SOE network, where she had the leading position, being the only woman in such a role. Her fiancé helped her organize the network, which was called "Wrestler," and they collaborated very closely with another network created to fill the gap: Shipwright, which was headed by Amédée Maingard. He was the wireless operator of the dissolved Stationer network and had escaped arrest by pure luck himself the day Southgate had been captured. Pearl's new code name for the mission was "Pauline," and her network was again active in the Indre department of central France.

On June 11, five days after D-Day, Pearl's network's headquarters at the Les Souces château was attacked by German troops. She hid in a nearby wheat field, just having time to hide the money she kept in the château for the mission. She hid all day until nightfall, while the German soldiers destroyed all the equipment of the network. The Wrestler network was hit, among other targets, that day, and the German operation was not a small one. The German troops had come with 56 trucks, as Henri Cornioley said later, so they were a much larger force than the Maquis could confront. During that operation, the Germans killed 32 Maquis in the surrounding areas and destroyed many weapons and materials. However, they didn't care about searching for more maquis or SOE agents, as it seems that their goal was mostly to eliminate weapons that could reinforce the Allied forces. The Allied armies had landed and marched in Normandy against the Nazi forces, so the German troops in France could not be thorough or invest much time in going after the SOE agents and maquis.

That meant Pearl wasn't killed or arrested that day, and her network continued to make a significant contribution to the Allies' war effort. However, the situation seemed desperate after the German raid had left her and her network without guns or wireless sets, so they couldn't even ask for help from London. Everything seemed lost. However, Pearl Witherington would not give in. With great determination, she insisted and found her way to another SOE agent in the region, Philippe de Vomécourt, who was at Saint-Viâtre and still had a radio. Pearl, who got there on a bicycle, requested help and supplies from the SOE headquarters in England, and thankfully, three airplanes dropped supplies for her network on June 24. Not only that, but the progress of the Allies on the front had meanwhile created more enthusiasm among the local youth, who joined the resistance in great numbers during June. By the time Pearl's network was back in business, the maquis in the area had reached around 3,500, and the SOE provided even more supplies, with 60 airdrops full of arms and other equipment. The arrangements worked well. During the crucial days in June of 1944, while the Battle of Normandy was steaming ahead, the networks of Pearl and Maingard collaborated for a combined 800 sabotages that damaged railway lines and caused interruptions, making transport and transfers from Paris to Bordeaux much more difficult for the Germans.

Success came from Pearl's organizational skills, too. She and her fiancé Henri had created four groups of maquis with different leaders so they could be more effective. Moreover, Pearl requested a military officer be sent to help her by leading the Maquis of the region directly at the military level, as she coordinated the actions with the broader Allied strategic plans. That finally happened on July 25, with the arrival of Colonel Francois Pedriset. Pearl was clever enough to understand that a French Colonel would be more credible for the local resistance members to follow without hesitation or question than a female British SOE agent, so she focused on doing the job instead of pretending to be bossy.

## Frustration and Recognition

As the Allies were pushing the Germans out of France in the last days of August 1944, the French authorities were retaking control of the territory and also the various armed units of the resistance scattered throughout the country. Their new name was the French Forces of the Interior. So, the French ordered Pearl's network of maquis to position themselves in the Forest of Gatine to obstruct the German forces' movement from the South to the North of France and the uniting of their army units. Pearl disagreed with that choice, but she participated and moved with her network's maquis. A few days later, a German force of almost 20,000 soldiers ended up in a desperate position, and its leadership decided to surrender. This awesome news was disappointing and frustrating for Pearl and the Maquis because

German General Botho Elster insisted on surrendering officially to a regular army and not to the Maquis. He thought the Maquis would not respect the war rules and that it would be more honorable to surrender to an official army.

So, he negotiated and came to an agreement with General Robert C. Macon of the U.S. Army. In addition, the Germans and the Americans did not even invite any Maquis' representatives to the meeting for the surrender negotiations, held on September 11 and concluding officially on September 16. The German general signed the surrender on that day at Beaugency Bridge.

That lack of recognition and respect from enemies and allies made Pearl mad. Making matters even worse, after the surrender, the American soldiers were friendly toward the German soldiers, offering them oranges and chocolates. The maquis didn't take it well either. Having lived in harsh conditions for the years of German occupation, witnessing that magnanimous American behavior toward the former occupiers was not easy for them to stomach. Furthermore, they felt they were snubbed as the Americans and the Germans hadn't invited them to be part of the formal surrender ceremony because both of them recognized each other as soldiers, but not the maquis and the SOE agents. All that made many members of the French Resistance furious, and it resulted in tearing down American flags and writing letters of protest in newspapers.

Frustrating as those events were to Pearl and others, they were nevertheless minor details. The crucial historical event was the Allies were marching victoriously in France, and the Nazi dominion was dwindling on all fronts. Pearl's mission was completed with great success, and on September 21, 1944, the SOE headquarters ordered her and everybody with her to return to Britain.

Another important event for Pearl came roughly a month later, when she finally married her fiancé Henri Cornioley on October 26, in the Kensington Register Office; the war failed to separate them, and they would live together for the rest of their lives, also having a daughter Claire. Pearl was awarded the civil division Member of the Order of the British Empire (MBE), but she refused to accept the medal as she thought it was downplaying her service, which was military and not civil. Again, she felt frustrated for not being recognized as a real soldier, like in the last days of her mission in France, and contested that she was in the field, not behind a desk all day. Soldier Pearl got what she wanted and deserved shortly after, accepting a proper military MBE, and years later, she was also promoted to Commander of the Order of the British Empire.

During her long life, she remained attached to her WWII contribution, as we can see from her emotion when she was finally given her parachute wings at the age of 92. Normally, one should have done at least five jumps, four during the training and one operational, while she had done three during the training and one when she landed in France in 1943. However, the one missing jump was not her fault, as the necessities of the war at that time had shortened the training periods. Pearl had to do the operational jump with less training than normal, and she considered it an injustice that she didn't receive her parachute wings for 63 years. Finally, in April 2006, that injustice was corrected. She died at 93 on February 24, 2008, in the Loire Valley in France, after a full and happy life.

Pearl Witherington was awarded the French Legion of Honor, and in 1991, she and her husband were among those who contributed to the Valençay SOE Memorial that was being created. She also had a distinguished professional career after the war, working for the World Bank.

# Chapter 6:

# Krystyna Skarbek—"Christine Granville"

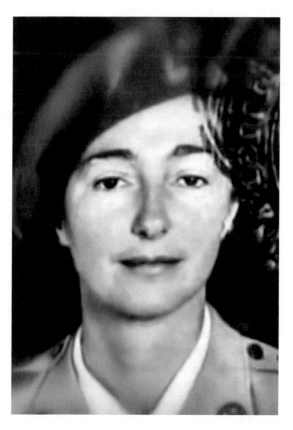

*Christine did not live, or love, as most people do. She lived boundlessly, as generous as she could be cruel, prepared to give her life at any moment for a worthy cause, but*

*rarely sparing a thought for the many casualties that fell in her wake.* —Clare Mulley, *The Spy Who Loved: The Secrets and Lives of Christine Granville*

Krystyna Skarbek was again an agent of the British Special Operations Executive. However, unlike the previous four women, she was Polish, and she operated not only in France but also in Poland under Nazi occupation.

# Early Years

Born Maria Krystyna Janina Skarbek, known also by the name Christine Granville, Krystyna was born in Warsaw, Poland, on May 1, 1908. Her father was a Count, Count Jerzy Skarbek, and her mother's name was Stefania née Goldfeder. Krystyna's father was a Catholic known for his debts and his luxurious lifestyle, while her mother came from a wealthy family of Jewish heritage. Krystyna had a very close relationship with her father, who was a banker, and they shared a love for horses, riding, and skiing, frequently visiting the Tatra Mountains in Poland.

Krystyna lost her father when she was 22 years old, in 1930, ten years after the family had moved to Warsaw due to financial problems. To make things worse, the Goldfeders, her mother's family, were almost broke, as their once mighty financial business had critically deteriorated. Krystyna then proved her responsibility and independence, wanting to relieve her mother by finding a job as a car dealer for FIAT, the Italian automobile enterprise. Unfortunately, her career in the automobile industry was not going to last. She soon became ill because she couldn't stand the fumes, and her doctor advised her to live in a clean-air environment.

That was how the Tatra Mountains, the place where she loved to ski, became central to her life again. There, Krystyna met Jerzy Giżycki, a very adventurous and fascinating guy originating from a wealthy Polish family who had abandoned his home at 14 after he argued with his father and lived in the United States, where he worked as a cowboy and was also a gold digger. Then, he went to several other countries, many of them in Africa, making himself a living as a writer. Krystyna met Jerzy when he saved her from a bad fall while skiing in the Tatra Mountains. The two got married on November 2, 1938, in Warsaw.

It was not her first marriage, as she had married already in 1930, with that marriage ending quickly. Moreover, another relationship ended before marriage because her fiancé's mother rejected the possibility as Krystyna was broke. Fortunately, Krystyna was an attractive young woman who was also runner-up in the 1930 Miss Poland beauty contest and was lucky enough to meet the right guy. This eccentric and brilliant, self-sufficient man didn't care about his wife's financial state, and he always managed to find opportunities and grab them. Right after their marriage, Jerzy received a proposal to become consul general of Poland in Ethiopia, apparently thanks to his relations and knowledge of Africa. He accepted, and the couple moved to Ethiopia. However, his job and their presence in Africa was not going to last for long, as some months later, in September 1939, Poland was occupied and cut in half by Nazi Germany in the West and Communist Soviet Union in the East. Under these circumstances, Jerzy and Krystyna decided to leave Ethiopia and the diplomatic job and head to Britain, and they settled in London in October 1939.

# Entering the War

Krystyna was eager to fight against those who had occupied her country since the beginning. She immediately asked the British authorities for a post from where she could actively fight against the common enemy of Poland and Britain since Britain had officially declared war on Germany right after the Wehrmacht invaded Poland. Although she had no history of being involved in the military or being an agent, the Secret Intelligence Service paid attention to her request after a British journalist she knew, Frederick Augustus Voigt, talked to them about her. The SIS was indeed fascinated by her and hired her very quickly, seeing that this Polish girl was fearless, a great adventuress with excellent skiing skills, and a flaming patriot.

Soon after, on December 21, 1939, Krystyna arrived in Budapest, Hungary, as an agent of SIS, pretending to be a journalist. From Hungary, she passed to Poland through her loved Tatra Mountains in February 1940, after she convinced Jan Marusarz, a Polish skier at the Olympics, to come with her. For the whole year, she was between Poland and Hungary, trying to collect intelligence. During that period, she met a Polish army officer named Andrzej Kowerski who was extracting personnel and gathering information. Krystyna had met him years ago, and again just before the war started at the Tatra mountains and was able to collaborate with him successfully. They got together a network of couriers who regularly transferred reports with pieces of information from Poland to Budapest.

Furthermore, after MI6 requested it, they created a group that surveilled the traffic between Romania and Germany. They kept the roads, rivers, and trains under scrutiny, and by doing so, to Krystyna's credit, they managed to provide information regarding the transport of oil from the Ploiesti oilfields in Romania to Germany, which was essential for the Germans. At a more personal level, Krystyna tried to convince her mother to leave Warsaw and flee to another country, but Countess Stefania Skarbek was teaching children French, and she wanted to continue her job in Warsaw, so she refused.

In January 1941, Krystyna was arrested along with Kowerski by the Hungarian police, and they were interrogated by the German Gestapo. That was because Hungary, although neutral, was at the time practically aligned with Germany. Being in the hands and the cells of the Gestapo was perhaps the worst thing that could happen, yet Krystyna found a way out. She knew well the symptoms of tuberculosis because her father had died from that disease, and she had been mistakenly diagnosed with it years before, so she pretended that she had tuberculosis, causing her tongue to bleed by biting it so she could spit blood. The German doctor fell for the trick and diagnosed her with it for the second time in her life, adding that it was terminal. The trick worked, and the Gestapo let her and Kowerski go.

# A New Name and a Great Adventure

Nevertheless, Hungary was not a safe country anymore. Even though the Germans released them, they kept them under surveillance. There is a possibility that they pretended to believe Krystyna had tuberculosis to let her go and try to get more information by following her rather than by interrogating her. It could all have been a case of spy games; who knows? Krystyna and Kowerski were aware of that and knew they had to go. They did so with the help of the British Ambassador in Hungary, who gave them British passports with fake identities. Krystyna's name on the passport was Christine Granville, and that's where that second name we mentioned in the title and the beginning of the chapter came from. This wasn't just an alias for the war as Krystyna would choose to keep it as her new name for the rest of her life. So, we will respect her will, and we'll call her Christine from now on (like Cassius Klay/Muhammad Ali).

We don't want to speculate, but maybe the fact that the passport cut seven years from Christine's age, mentioning a birth date of 1915 instead of the real one, 1908, played a role in her preference for this new identity. The name they chose for Kowerski's British passport was Anthony Kennedy, which is also funny when we think what that surname would mean for the US and the world some years later. The British Ambassador's name was Owen O'Malley, and his wife was Ann Bridge, a novelist. They both helped Christine and Kowerski flee from Hungary to Britain.

However, that didn't mean the escape was easy. Christine had to be extremely careful, and she was transported to Yugoslavia from Hungary in the trunk of the Ambassador's Chrysler, driven by an Embassy driver. At the same time, Kowerski passed the borders driving his own car. After they got into Yugoslavia and met again, they went to Belgrade, where they later visited Ambassador O'Malley. Here they could relax and have some fun being entertained in the nightlife of the Yugoslavian capital. Then, towards the end of February 1941, Christine and Kowerski went to Sofia, Bulgaria, another ally of Germany. There, they performed a serious intelligence mission as in the midst of the Nazis, they met Aidan Crawley, the British air attaché, and gave him a very important microfilm, previously given to them by Polish agents. The microfilm contained shocking images that proved the Germans were preparing to invade the Soviet Union, as there were photos of German military units moving and gathering secretly near the borders.

That information has great historical importance, as it was one of the first intelligence reports that gave notes about the invasion of the Soviet Union in what would become the biggest front of WWII, the Eastern Front. It's compelling that the microfilm eventually got to Winston Churchill's hands, who was the British Prime Minister since May 1940. Churchill didn't believe immediately that Hitler was planning to attack Stalin, but after he received more reports and information that indicated the same thing, he accepted the notion and later even informed the Soviet Union's government about the imminent German invasion, which indeed occurred on June 22, 1941.

After they handed over the microfilm with the critical information, Christine and Kowerski traveled to Istanbul, Turkey, where they met with some Poles in March 1941. Christine's job was to make sure that courier routes between the two countries, Turkey and Poland, would remain open and active. But the most important point of this trip was when Christine and Kowerski met with her husband, Jerzy Giżycki, who, in addition to what we said about him earlier, was also very tall, large, and not someone you would pick a fight with. Nevertheless, when Christine told Jerzy she loved Kowerski, it seemed that they came to a good understanding, and they were all dedicated to the cause, so Jerzy accepted to move to Budapest in Hungary and work at Christine's old post as the contact between the Polish resistance and the British intelligence and government.

Christine and Kowerski continued on in his car, which was an Opel, and they entered Syria and then Lebanon, countries under French control, which by that time meant under German-controlled Vichy France. They made it to Mandatory Palestine, which was British-controlled territory, and then, in May 1941, they finally arrived in Cairo, Egypt, which belonged to the British Empire and was one of the most important administrative centers of the Allies during the war. At the same time in May 1941, the Greek government arrived in Cairo also. This was after the German invasion of Greece at the end of a seven-month war which had begun with the defeated Italian invasion of Greece in late October 1940 and then the German invasion of the country on April 6, 1941.

However, when Christine and Kowerski arrived in Cairo, the British and Allied officers did not receive them well. The fact that they had got visas so easily through countries controlled by Vichy France, being Nazi Germany, seemed suspicious to the Allied intelligence. Some Polish agents thought the only way they could have made it to Cairo was by working for the Nazis. There were other reasons for suspicion, too, around Christine. To make matters worse, an officer of the SOE named Peter Wilkinson arrived in Cairo and dismissed them from service on June 15. The only consolation was that they continued to receive a very small salary, which was not enough to live on. Obviously, it meant that the British intelligence was not sure about their collaboration with the enemy and was suspicious enough to put their activities on hold until things became clearer.

Christine joined the First Aid Nursing Yeomanry (FANY), which was a women's charity organization that was also the cover for several female SOE agents. There, she impressed her officer Gwendolin Lees and an SOE officer named Patrick Howarth, and in this way, the doors of the SOE opened again for her. As they welcomed her back, her first job was training agents, and she had not yet returned to active roles. That would happen with a mission to France. The Polish government, also stationed in Cairo at that time, continued to suspect her as a possible Nazi agent, so she couldn't participate in missions in her country.

The previous ladies we have spoken of were all members of the F Section that launched operations from Great Britain into France. Christine was based in Algiers as a member of the AMF Section, which was created just before Operation Torch, the massive Anglo-American landing in North Africa in 1942. The headquarters of the AMF Section was in Algiers and not in London like those in F Section. The AMF Section focused mainly on Southern France instead of the North and on securing the supply of the armies in North Africa.

# In France

Christine parachuted into Southern France in the early hours of July 7, 1944, and joined the SOE Jockey network. Their mission would be to organize the local French resistance, the maquis of the South, in order to help the imminent attack of the Allies on the French South after the success of Operation Overlord in the North. The Allies' operation in the South would be called Operation Dragoon. Operation Dragoon would be similar to D-Day, with Allied forces landing in the region of Provence in Southern France.

The Jockey network's base was in the Vercors Plateau, and its chief was Francis Cammaerts, who interestingly was a Belgian-British pacifist before the war and obviously had to come to terms with the real world the hard way. Christine became his courier, which was not as safe as one may think. Actually, the previous courier had been arrested and then executed by the Germans, which is why they needed her to fill the courier role.

When Christine arrived in France, there was a massive need for supplies for her network the SOE units and maquis. She started collecting light arms and other supplies that landed by parachute at night. A week later, the largest landing of supplies and arms to the French Resistance occurred. By mid-July, the Northern front was going well for the Allies. General Charles de Gaulle, who was the president of the provisional French government and the leader of the resistance, thought the time had come for an all in battle against the German occupying forces. The maquis agreed. De Gaulle delivered a speech that created great enthusiasm, and nobody heard Cammaerts, who instead thought the French resistance forces were not yet strong enough and ready for a battle like that. The result was a tough defeat of the rebellion, but at least Cammaerts and Christine managed to escape the battlefield alive on July 22 and settled at Seyne-les-Alpes.

Christine was given a new mission on the border of France and Italy, where she helped organize and get supplies to the resistance groups there. It took her three weeks to cover the distance, passing through the Alps on foot while she carried food and hand grenades in her rucksack, and finally, she met French resistance leaders and SOE agents, some of whom were already her friends. Furthermore, because of her Polish nationality, Christine took on another risky mission. She approached the Polish soldiers who had been conscripted by the Germans and were stationed in the area and tried to convince them to desert the Wehrmacht. They were at a fortress near the Col de Larche

Mountain pass, which the resistance aimed to occupy. The garrison had 150 soldiers, and 63 of them were Polish. Christine understood that if she could convince the Polish soldiers to join the resistance, the fortress would more easily fall. Using her magnetic personality, her effort had great success, as the soldiers agreed to join the resistance, and she gave them instructions on what would happen and what they should do. After a few days, a maquis unit and SOE agents attacked the fortress, and the commanding officer surrendered, seeing that a great number of the garrison had turned against the Germans.

That was mid-August 1944 when Operation Dragoon was about to begin. At the same time, Cammaerts and two other SOE agents were captured by the Germans at one of the Gestapo roadblocks in Digne. Christine was not going to abandon them. This time, she stormed back to Col de Larche, and on August 15, the same day as the landing of the Allies in Southern France was beginning, she was outside the prison where Cammaerts was held. The way she confirmed his presence there has to be told! She walked around the prison's walls, quietly singing the popular American song "Frankie and Johnny," which they both loved, and he responded by singing it, too. So, Christine found a way to talk to Captain Albert Schenck, who was responsible for the prisoners, and told him she was Cammaert's wife. That was not the best lie she used. She told him that she was also General Montgomery's niece. That meant the officer would have had a very hard time if Cammaerts and the other SOE agents were harmed in prison. Then, a threat always works best if money accompanies it. Christine promised Schenck that if he released the prisoners, she would give him two million francs.

She then talked with SOE headquarters, and they agreed to send her the money in the usual way, by parachute drop. She returned immediately to Digne with the money and talked again with Schenck, who, this time, had a Gestapo officer named Max Waem with him. He had the authority to release the prisoners. And so, he did, after talking with Christine for three hours. The fact that it was August 17, 1944, and the Allies were advancing closer to Digne helped a lot. Waem's main concern was to see what she could do to protect him after he had executed so many people during the war. Cammaerts and the other two prisoners, named Xan Fielding and Christian Sorensen, were released, with Waem burying his SS tunic. Just two days later, Digne was indeed liberated by the Allies. Schenck didn't get to enjoy the money as he was murdered, and it was never discovered who did it.

The last chapter of Christine's war adventures was again rather unusual. The maquis had captured the German garrison in Gap, and among the prisoners, there were hundreds of Polish soldiers, similar to the cases we saw previously. Christine and Cammarts went there, and she took a megaphone and told the Poles to join the Allies. After they agreed, she told them to strip off their German uniforms to prove it. The Polish soldiers did that willingly, but Brigadier General Frederic B. Butler had something to say about those unorthodox methods. Not only was he unimpressed, but he threatened to arrest Christine and Cammaerts to unless they left right away. He considered them "bandits," unworthy of working with a real army. Christine was furious! Fortunately, that wasn't the end of the story, as General Alexander Patch, who was Butler's superior, learned about them and was so impressed by them that he appointed them as a connection between the American troops and the French maquis. Christine and Cammaerts went on to Lyon and Paris, and her job in France concluded in September 1944, when she finally landed in London on a military plane.

# A Bitter Ending

The aftermath of the war was strange for Christine. The Allies had won against Nazi Germany, but Poland was not truly liberated as it had fallen under Soviet rule. A Communist pro-Soviet regime was established, and it would last for decades. Christine found herself in a position where she couldn't return to her country, and she didn't have any money since the British intelligence gave her a month's salary and dismissed her right after the end of the war. To add to that she was already separated from her husband as she had told him she loved Kowerski, and they officially divorced in 1946. Her mother had been captured as a Jew by the Nazis in 1942 after refusing to follow her daughter and leave and was lost forever in the Pawiak prison of Warsaw. This story is like a tale with tragic shifts: the architect of that prison was Fryderyk Skarbek, Christine's great-great-uncle, in the mid-19th century. The tale goes on: he was Frédéric Chopin's godfather.

Again, adventure was ahead for Christine, but this time, it wouldn't be glorious. She didn't want to ask for help, so instead, she worked as a waitress, a salesperson, and a telephone operator. Then, she sailed with ocean liners, becoming a cabin steward. On the ship Ruahine, the captain asked the crew to wear medals they had been awarded during the war, if any. Christine had received the George Medal, and she was awarded Officer of the Order of the British Empire and the French Croix de Guerre. Needless to say, all that impressed the passengers greatly. Unfortunately, it also created resentment toward her from the rest of the crew, and their behavior became very bad. Another steward defended her, and she probably had a relationship with him. But Christine was very unlucky. Her new lover was obsessed with her and began treating her badly. She left him and returned to London, where she worked as a steward. On June 14, 1952, she booked into the Shelbourne Hotel. There, on June 15, 1952, her obsessed former lover, Dennis Muldowney, murdered her with a knife. He was sentenced to death and hanged on September 30.

It's so tragic to think that Christine didn't get any support from either her country or from the country she helped to win the war. While she was given the highest possible honors, they began a sequence of events that led to her unjust, premature death. Maybe the most important honor was the love and respect shown to her and her memory by those with whom she had shared the heroic and glorious adventures of WWII. Xan Fielding dedicated his 1954 book "Hide and Seek" to her memory, while Francis Cammaerts gave her name, Christine, to his daughter.

# Chapter 7:

# Vera Atkins—The Unseen Warrior

*A woman with a voice is by definition a strong woman.* –Melinda Gates

# Early Years

Vera Atkins was raised in what we would call a multicultural and cosmopolitan environment, along with her two brothers. She was born in Galați, a city in Romania, to Max Rosenberg and Zefra Hilda, and her name was then Vera May Rosenberg. Her father was a wealthy German-Jewish businessman, and her mother British-Jewish. Her mother's maiden name was Atkins, which Vera later adopted.

So, German, British, Jew, in Romania, and that's only the beginning. Vera went to Paris where she studied languages briefly at the University of Sorbonne. Later, she continued her education at a finishing school in Lausanne, Switzerland, where she practiced skiing. Then again, in London, where she attended a secretarial college. Moreover, her status gave Vera the opportunity to interact with people of international backgrounds starting as a young girl, and interestingly, one of the people she met was the German ambassador in Bucharest, Friedrich Werner von der Schulenburg, who was an opposer of the Nazi ideology and regime. In Romania, she also met several other diplomats and members of British intelligence.

# "James Bond" and Winston Churchill

Vera began working as a translator and a representative of an oil company, which is not a surprise due to all the languages she spoke and her experience in many countries. But her promising life and career as a young woman in Romania and continental Europe would not last. Already before the war broke out in 1937, her family had to leave for Great Britain due to growing financial problems. The situation was becoming difficult for people with Jewish heritage or for anybody else on the continent.

Vera and her family were even more aware of the situation, given their social background and acquaintances. So, it was no surprise that Vera's first job in Britain was focused on Nazism and intelligence. Her job was to travel all around Europe to find evidence about Germany and Nazism and the rising threat they represented. Vera worked for Sir William Stephenson, a Canadian spymaster who would be the head of British Security Coordination and one of the principal figures who helped move the American public opinion from its support for non-involvement to being more open to direct American involvement in the war. It becomes even better: according to Ian Fleming himself, the James Bond character and initial novels were modeled on Sir Stephenson. To make our story even more intriguing and exciting is the fact that the person who had asked for those investigations was Winston Churchill himself, and he fully intended to use the findings in his strategies. By this time, Winston Churchill was a solitary and not-so-popular political figure on the sidelines of his party and British politics.

## Top Intelligence Agent During the War

In September 1939, just after the beginning of World War II, Vera's first mission for British intelligence was in Poland, helping three Polish cryptologists, Marian Rejewski, Jerzy Różycki, and Henryk Zygalski, flee their country. As members of the Polish Cipher Bureau, they had decrypted the German Enigma codes, and things were becoming dangerous for them. A few days before the German invasion of Poland, in late August 1939, Vera traveled through Greece and Romania to get to Poland with another agent named Colin Gubbins. However, apparently, their effort was in vain, as the Polish cryptologists had already been transferred to France by the French intelligence.

Vera's second attempt to impact the ongoing war wasn't completely successful either. She went to the Netherlands in 1940 on a personal mission to bribe an officer of the Abwehr, the German military intelligence in the Netherlands, in order for her cousin Fritz to get a passport and leave Romania. She managed to get her cousin out of the country thanks to the bribe, but she became trapped in the Netherlands herself. In Poland in 1939, she escaped the German invasion by a few days, but in the Netherlands, she didn't. This time, she was still in the country when the Wehrmacht invaded it on May 10, 1940, and occupied it almost immediately. Dutch military resistance, similar to that of Denmark and other countries, was practically nonexistent, as those countries surrendered before even fighting. Vera was trapped in the Netherlands and had to hide, but that wasn't easy, and it was even harder to find a way out. Finally, towards the end of 1940, she found help from a Belgian resistance group and returned to England. Vera kept this personal mission and adventure secret from the British intelligence as she had practically collaborated with the Abwehr.

In February 1941, Vera joined the F Section of the SOE. Although she was still not a British citizen, they hired her as a secretary, which was fine but not what she wanted. Through working hard and showing how capable she was Vera soon became assistant to the F Section chief Colonel Maurice Buckmaster, who, again, we've already met. Buckmaster valued and trusted her abilities, honesty, and organizational skills. So, although she was formally just a secretary, Vera worked as an intelligence officer and the most immediate and close collaborator of the Chief of F Section.

Her most important role as the right hand of the F Section's leader was to receive the decoded transmissions of the SOE agents, recruit and supervise the training of new female agents and spies, and then deploy them to France. That function included the responsibility of managing those women, meaning she took care of their documentation for the missions, the supplies they needed, and the payment of their salaries. She was the one who communicated with their families and had to inform them when something good or bad happened.

Vera often stayed at the office until late at night and worked very hard for British intelligence. Everything we have mentioned or will mention in this book that is related to the SOE, especially the F Section, has something to do with Vera. She prepared, coordinated, and supervised everything the agents, especially the female agents, did in the field during those years, receiving their reports. So, even though there are not many exciting spy stories in her story, Vera's crucial role cannot be highlighted enough.

# Accusations and Controversies

However, that didn't prevent her from facing some harsh criticism and suspicion about her real role. At least a few times, agents died after mistakes made by the SOE central. There were questions about why she and Buckmaster did not retract agents whose networks had been compromised, and they were at risk.

One of the most known cases of controversy is the one related to Noor Inayat Khan, which we saw in chapter 4. Sonia Olschanezky was a locally recruited SOE agent and she had managed to send the SOE headquarters a message informing them that Noor had been captured. She did so through her fiancé, who was another SOE wireless operator named Jaques Weil. As we said, unfortunately, Buckmaster didn't believe the information, probably because he didn't know who Sonia was. The point was that they continued to accept messages of "Madeleine," Noor's code name, as authentic for months while the German military intelligence sent them. That mistake resulted in serious damage as several agents were sent to a compromised network, where they were easily captured and killed by the Germans. Vera has been accused of being responsible for those deaths and failures because she received all those messages and accepted them as really coming from Noor. She also mistakenly thought later that Sonia was Noor and not a different agent. However, Vera probably knew nothing about the initial message, so she shouldn't be blamed for what happened next. In any case, it seems there had been confusion about members who were trained and registered in the SOE headquarters. and locally recruited members who weren't trained or registered.

It should be added that the great failure of the SOE did not happen in France, where Vera's F Section operated, but in the Netherlands and Belgium, where the N Section and the T Section operated. The Abwerh had great success between 1942 and 1944, compromising and practically dismantling all the SOE networks, as they captured their radio operators and got their codes and keys. The Germans called that counterintelligence operation *Englandspiel*, England game. It's not clear why, but the SOE decided not to inform the F Section that the N and T Sections were so heavily compromised. Indeed, Vera and

Buckmaster didn't learn of this until after the end of the war. Every SOE operator in the Lower Countries was turned into a "zombie," their names and codes were used by the German intelligence to create confusion and mislead the British.

Nothing similar happened in France. The service's function and operations were not heavily comprised by the loss of agents. Although the *Sicherheitsdienst*, the German military intelligence in France headed by Hans Kieffer, was very capable and efficient, the SOE agents working with the French Resistance had a generally positive impact. They had a successful presence in France until the end of the war and helped the Allies liberate the country in the summer of 1944, as we have seen in several examples so far, and we'll also see in the following chapters. Buckmaster and Vera should get credit for this success since they were the head office of the SOE F Section.

## Searching for the Missing Agents

Vera was not decorated by the British right after the war, as the accusations and controversies weighed on her, and there were also suspicions about her being a German or Soviet spy. Her personal mission in the Netherlands in 1940, of which she never spoke, and her secrecy played a role in giving her a sinister aura to some of the intelligence officers. We mustn't forget that she was also a foreigner, coming from a country that became Hitler's ally, and as a Romanian citizen, she didn't receive British citizenship until 1944.

After the war, when she traveled to France and Germany to try to trace the missing agents of the F Section, some saw this as an attempt to cover her failures or contacts with the enemy. The government didn't like her personal mission either, but they changed their minds when the extent and the ferocity of the Nazi crimes began to come to light. We need to remember that during the war, it was not clear what the Nazis were doing. People rarely had a clear picture of what was really happening in the concentration camps. When we now think about history, knowing the outcome, we don't realize that it was unknown to those who actually lived the events in real life.

Vera received official support in her attempt to find out what had happened to the missing SOE agents and bring Nazi criminals to justice. MI6 funded her research since the SOE was dissolved by the end of 1945. Now, she was a British citizen and an officer of the Women's Auxiliary Air Force. She began her investigation in January 1946, and she concluded one year later. In that period, she traced 117 of the 118 agents of the F Section that had disappeared into enemy territory without anyone knowing what had happened to them. Unfortunately, all of them were dead. Fourteen of them were women, among them Noor Inayat Khan, whose story we've seen in a previous chapter, and Violette Szabo, whose story we'll see in the following chapter. Vera certified exactly how 12 of those 14 women died, and she didn't stop at that, but she pushed for them to be recognized as killed in action and not civilians who died in prison and for them to be offered the official recognition of the British government. That's how, thanks to Vera's efforts, Violette and Noor got their posthumous George Crosses.

Finally, half a century later, Vera was also decorated by the British. She was accepted as CBE, i.e., Commander of the Order of British Empire, the British order of chivalry. That was in 1997, during the Queen's Birthday Honours. However, in 1948, she had already received decorations from the French after the war, when she was awarded the Croix de Guerre, and again in 1987, when the French government selected her as Knight of the Legion of Honour.

Vera died at 92 on June 24, 2000. She was active until late in her life, and we can see how dear her story and role as the unofficial F Section leader were to her and how she cared about her agents. She wrote to the Daily Telegraph in 1996. At almost 90 years of age, Vera insisted and defended her controversial decision to send Noor to France, which, as we saw, was challenged and questioned. Vera mentioned some outstanding points of Noor's story, claiming that her operating as an agent proved she was capable, and her value should never be doubted, even though, like many others, she was captured and killed by the Nazis.

# Chapter 8:

# Violette Szabo—"Louise"

*Courage doesn't always roar. Sometimes courage is the quiet voice at the end of the day saying, 'I will try again tomorrow.'* –Mary Anne Radmacher

# A Tomboy

Violette Szabo, born Violette Bushell in Paris on June 26, 1921, was the only daughter of her family. She had four brothers, one of whom was older, and her parents were Charles George Bushell and Reine Blanche Leroy. Violette's parents had a romantic story. Her father was a driver for the British Army in France during World War I, and there he met her mother, who was a dressmaker. They fell in love, and after the war, they got married and went to live in London. They weren't a very wealthy family. In London, Violette's father was a taxi driver, and he also worked as a salesman in a car company before he opened a shop.

Things became worse after the 1929 crash and the Great Depression. Violette and one of her brothers even had to move to Picardy, France, to live with their mother's French aunt for a while. They returned to London in 1932-33, and Violette went to school in Brixton. Interestingly, while in France, she got so used to speaking in French that it was difficult for her to return to English. Of course, she quickly became familiar with the English language again in school, but she maintained an aura that fascinated her schoolmates, excited by the fact that she could speak another language so well. At home, except for her English father, they used to speak both languages, as the mother had taught the kids French.

Violette's father taught her other things, like shooting a gun, something she did with great accuracy. Violette, as a girl, generally loved activities that were more often connected with boys, although she was not tall at all (just 5'3" as an adult). Nevertheless, she played all the time with her four brothers plus many male cousins. So, she was good at bicycling, ice skating, and, in general, playing sports.

It seems Violette had a very independent spirit, too. When she was just 14 years old, she went to work for a corset maker based in Kensington. Then, she found other jobs, working at a retailer in Oxford Street and in a department store in Brixton. And then, the war came.

# Trying to Help the War Effort

It didn't take long before Violette decided she wanted to fight for her country as her father had done in the previous war. In early 1940, she joined the Women's Land Army, which was a civilian organization founded during WWI to help Britain's war effort by putting women to work in the fields which allowed more men to join the real army and fight at the fronts. However, Violette was not satisfied with this role, as she wasn't interested in agriculture, and she wanted to do something closer to the real military and war effort. She returned to London and found a job in an armaments factory based in Acton.

On July 14, 1940, while Paris and France had already fallen to the Germans, in London, the Bastille Day parade was held. Violette was there, and she met a noncommissioned French officer, Étienne Szabo. So, that's where her surname came from. Étienne was 31 years old, had Hungarian origins, and was a member of the Foreign Legion. Violette fell in love with him immediately, and they got married extremely quickly, 5 weeks later, on August 21, while she was still 19 years old. Those happy days lasted just a week, after which Violette's husband had to leave for Senegal, where the Free French of General Charles De Gaulle was launching an attack against Vichy France's forces at Dakar. In 1941, he joined the Free French forces in South Africa, where, in collaboration with British troops, they prepared more campaigns against Vichy France's forces, fighting in Eritrea and Syria during the same year.

Violette, now Violette Szabo, wanting to find a way to contribute to the war effort, entered the Auxiliary Territorial Service (ATC) on September 11, 1941. That was pretty much the real deal for a woman at this time, the beginning of the women's branch of the British Army. Its functions were, as it says, auxiliary, but as the war went on and there was an increasing need for more people, women were used in positions closer to the actual battles, such as anti-aircraft, military police, and radar operators. Indeed, after her training, Violette was appointed to one of the first anti-aircraft crews, which included women. Then, she passed a second training, and she specialized in becoming a gunner at Frodsham, Cheshire. We can imagine that Violette was thrilled by these events now allowing her to really fight, and secondly, her job would be to point and shoot, which she loved to do since her father taught her as a little girl. Only now, it was a much bigger gun, and it wasn't a game but about defending Britain.

Violette stayed at Frodsham from December 1941 to February 1942, but then, something unexpected happened: she found out she was pregnant. That meant she couldn't continue her war efforts, and she returned to London. Four months later, on June 8, 1942, her daughter Tania was born. It was a happy moment for the young mother, but on the other hand, the war was always present, which meant that her husband was absent. Étienne was fighting now in North Africa, in one of the hottest fronts of the whole war, and in the two days that followed his daughter's birth, he valiantly fought against Rommel's Afrika Korps and, in particular, the 15th Panzer Division at Bir Hakeim, and eventually he had to escape from their heavy attack.

That escape was only temporary. On October 24, 1942, the second day of the historic Second Battle of El Alamein, Étienne Szabo was killed at Qaret el Himeimat, suffering deep chest wounds while leading his platoon in a diversionary attack. Violette was by then living near her father at South Morden, working in an aircraft factory. Perhaps she moved there so her father could help with her daughter. Her first priority was now her daughter, not the war. However, her husband's death filled her with despair and fury. When it was suggested that she join the SOE, she accepted. Now, the war was also personal.

# Member of the SOE

Violette passed the basic and then more specialized training from August to October 1943 after being selected in July 1943. Previously, she had been interviewed by Selwyn Jepson, the detective novelist who was a recruiter for the F Section, which, of course, was the one Violette joined. Her fluency in French and knowledge of the country, plus her previous experience in the ATS and the Women's Land Army, apparently made the SOE interested in her.

The reports on Violette were not enthusiastic but were somewhat positive, so she concluded her training at Beaulieu, Hampshire. Not without accidents, however, as she hurt her ankle and had to postpone the parachuting lessons, which she finally completed in February 1944. Since summer, she had learned fieldcraft, using weapons, navigating day and night, demolishing buildings, escaping, recognizing uniforms, using telecommunications, and cryptography.

Violette landed in France as a SOE agent in the Loire Valley in the early hours of April 6. With her was Philippe Liewer, who was the organizer of the SOE network she was going to work for, called Salesman. Violette would be his courier, and her cover name was Corinne Reine Leroy, from the name of her mother. She was supposedly a commercial secretary, and her code name was "Louise."

Violette's first mission was to go to Rouen and the coastal area of Dieppe to try to obtain information and identify enemy movements in the region. Recently, the SOE headquarters received a message from another network called Author, advising them that many of the initial 120 agents of the Salesman network had been exposed and arrested. Violette had to discover what was really happening. After a while, she understood that the Salesman network was totally compromised, and the situation was even worse than they imagined. The network practically didn't exist anymore, and they had to leave immediately and return to England if they wanted to avoid being captured themselves. They turned back at the end of April, and Violette's escape flight was also very dangerous as they were hit by German anti-aircraft. Nevertheless, Violette's first mission was not a total failure. During the time she spent in Rouen and Dieppe, she managed to investigate and return with reports about the factories that produced military products for the German armies.

The Allied invasion of Normandy had just begun when Violette returned to France in the first hours of June 8. She landed near Limoges together with three more agents. They were going to work for the network Salesman II, which was headed again by Liewer. His new network was active in the French department of Haute Vienne, in the

Limousin region (now part of the Nouvelle-Aquitaine area). Violette's mission would be to coordinate local French resistance groups that were trying to hamper the Germans' communications and harass their troops, creating problems and sabotaging, in order to help the Allies advance at this crucial front. This time, her cover name was Mme Villeret from Nantes, the widow of an antique dealer.

When Liewer arrived in the region, he realized that the local French Resistance members were not in peak condition and not capable of standing against the German troops. They lacked the training and leadership that they needed. Liewer decided to ask for help from the powerful SOE network called Digger, headed by Jacques Poirier, who collaborated with the much more war-ready French Resistance of the Correze and Dordogne departments. The maquis there were better trained and experienced, ready to accomplish missions and sabotages. The agent who was sent to deliver the message to Poirier was Violette.

Violette departed on the morning of June 10, accompanied by a Maquis leader. Liewer told her to cover the 62-mile distance on a bicycle. However, the Maquis, named Jacques Dufour, wanted to drive her halfway in a car, and he insisted on it. That was strange because the Germans had forbidden the use of cars after the Allies' landed in Normandy on June 6. Using the car made you an easy and certain target of the occupying forces. Yet, the Maquis wanted to go by car, thinking that the area was safe, and nothing could go wrong. Violette accepted it.

Unfortunately, things did not turn out as the maquis intended. As the car was approaching Salon-la-Tour, they met a German roadblock. Violette and Dufour found cover behind a tree, and he opened fire on the German soldiers. A third passenger, a young member of the resistance named Jean Bariaud, whom they had taken on the drive, managed to escape. On the contrary, an unlucky woman, frightened by the gun battle, came running out from a barn, and the German soldiers shot at her, killing her. Then, more German cars arrived, and the situation became desperate for Violette and Dufour. They ran towards a hill. But then, Violette's ankle, which had given her problems during the training and at other times in her life, betrayed her again. She fell and twisted it badly, something that made it impossible for her to go on. Dufour tried to help her, but she refused, telling him he had to flee.

As the Germans approached, Violette dragged herself to find cover behind an apple tree. From there, according to a version of the story, she began shooting at the Germans to provide cover for Dufour so he could get away. She killed at least one German soldier and wounded others, but she ran out of ammunition. Two German soldiers then arrested her, and an officer questioned her before the Germans took her and transferred her to Ravensbrück a couple of months later. That last part is certain. As for the story of the battle before her arrest, some authors and biographers confirm it, while others doubt it because there was no record of casualties in the German archives from that operation.

## Detention and Execution

Violette was put on a train on August 8, 1944, with other SOE agents and French resistance members whom the Germans had captured. By that time, the Allies were decisively winning in Northern France under General George Patton's leadership and were marching towards Paris. She was in chains with another female agent, Denise Bloch. The first destination was Reims, but an Allied raid during the journey made the German guards leave the train for a while to find cover. That gave the two young women the opportunity to go to a lavatory nearby and bring back water to the men who were held caged in the next wagon. Apparently, they were able to raise the caged men's spirits a little bit, and then, the Germans took the prisoners to a big barn for two nights. The two women washed some of their clothes and also talked about their experiences with other SOE agents.

The next stop was a camp at Saarbrücken, where the prisoners were transferred again by train. It was an awful place; the food and hygiene were terrible, and the prisoners had to stay there for 10 days. Then, the Germans divided them, and at the end of August, they took most of the women to Ravensbrück, one of the terrible Nazi concentration camps where many people lost their lives in those years of war and the destruction in Europe.

Violette didn't surrender. She kept making plans about escaping from the camp, maintaining high morale and helping the other prisoners feel a little bit better. She and others also helped to save the life of fellow prisoner Hortense Daman, a female member of the Belgian Resistance. Later, she was one of approximately 1,000 prisoners, all of them French women, who were transferred to work at the Heinkel aircraft manufacturing factory at Torgau. There, the French women revolted, protesting and refusing to work for the factory since it produced products for the German military, so the Germans made them work in the nearby vegetable cellar and fields.

The Germans punished the women who participated in the factory revolt: 250 were sent to the Königsberg camp. The conditions there were even tougher, as they had to dig a trench for a new railway and work on the construction of an airfield by clearing the ground, which was covered by ice and rocks. They also had to cut trees, and Violette volunteered for that work because, in the forest, the trees provided more protection from the severe winds. As we said, the conditions were extremely harsh. Violette wore just the clothes she had when they first transferred her to Germany, and all the prisoners had to work and sleep in freezing conditions with almost nothing to eat. Yet, prisoners who survived and narrated stories about the camp and Violette after the war said that her spirit never broke, and she kept hoping and trying to find a way to escape.

Violette and two other British women were transferred back to Ravensbrück roughly on January 20, 1945. There, the last and most brutal phase of punishment occurred, as they assaulted them and put them in solitary confinement. Two weeks later, on February 5, Violette was executed; however, the date is uncertain. They made her kneel down and killed her with a shot in the back of the head. German deputy commandant Johann Schwarzhuber reported in detail her execution to Vera Atkins, who, as we've seen in the previous chapter, made investigations and took depositions from Nazi war criminals in 1946, looking for the F Section lost agents. He was one of those present at the execution. Denise Bloch and Lilian Rolfe, Violette's friends during those months of captivity, were also executed on the same day.

Violette was awarded the George Cross medal on December 17, 1946. Her four-year-old daughter, Tania, received the cross from King George VI on January 28, 1947. In 1947, the French government also honored Violette with the *Croix de Guerre*, and again in 1973, when she was awarded the *Médaille de la Résistance*. The French government honored the posthumous *Croix de Guerre* to Violette's husband, Étienne Szabo, also, for dying while fighting bravely in North Africa in 1942. They are probably the most decorated couple of World War II. Violette, like the other F Section ladies we've seen, is also among the F Section SOE agents listed on the Valençay SOE Memorial, and the French Republic honors them for having died while working for the liberation of France from the Nazis.

# Chapter 9:

# Amy Elizabeth Thorpe—The

# Seductive Spy

*There were only three things SOE's agents could anticipate with confidence. That their parachutes would open, that their L-tablets would kill them, and that their*

*messages from London would be accurately encoded.* —Leo Marks, *Between Silk and Cyanide: A Codemaker's War*

The most common type of female spy in popular culture is the seductive spy. And let's be honest; this is what at least some have been waiting for since the beginning of the book, right? Finally, we are going to talk about the seductive spy. That's not to say that our previous female agents weren't attractive. On the contrary, they were beautiful; some were so young and charming. The difference is that Amy Elizabeth Thorpe, code name "Cynthia," had the classical characteristics of the seductive spy and is known in history as such, with her slim body, reportedly just a little bit taller than average, her blonde hair and large green eyes; most of all, her aristocratic attractiveness and resolve.

# Intense and Contentious Youth

Amy was born in Minneapolis, Minnesota, on November 22, 1910, to Cora Wells and George C. Thorpe. Her family was certainly not poor, and they were well-positioned in the military and political circles of the early American 20th century. Her father was a prominent Marine Corps officer, and her mother was the daughter of a senator in the state of Minnesota. Amy followed her parents to various assignments in Europe before her father retired in 1923. They settled in Washington, D.C. Her parents often also traveled to New York and Rhode Island, and they encouraged her to become familiar with a social scene that a person can rarely approach at such a young age. Being very attractive and speaking French from the time her family was in Europe, she had romantic relationships with various much older foreign diplomats as a very young woman.

Amy married one of those gentlemen before her 20th birthday, on April 29, 1930. His name was Arthur Pack. He was a second secretary at the Embassy of Great Britain in Washington and was 38 years old. There is a sad side to this story because, when they got married, she was pregnant, and they left the baby boy in Britain that year in a foster home. It's unclear why they made that decision. Did they simply not want children? Or was there another reason? Who was the child's father?

The following year, Pack was appointed to the British Embassy in Chile. They lived there for four years, and they had a daughter. Amy was charmed by South American Catholicism and converted to Catholicism. In 1935, Pack was appointed to Spain, which would be most important step in his career. It was the year before the start of the Spanish Civil War, which many consider to be the prelude to the Second World War. Amy explicitly and intensely took the side of General Francisco Franco's Catholic Nationalists against the Republicans. Maybe her being a newly converted Catholic played a role in that since the Republicans included anti-Catholic leftists and anarchists of Spain, where General Franco was the defender of the faith.

However, the most intriguing part of those years in Amy's story was again from her personal and sentimental life. First, she had an affair-or we should say, she seduced-a Catholic priest. And if this wasn't enough, she had another affair with a British diplomat. On the other side, her husband faced accusations of being a spy of the Republicans while he was supporting the Nationalists, too. Strangely, he reacted by finding Amy's priest after he undertook a dangerous trip, and then, he offered humanitarian help. Finally, while the Spanish Civil War would become ever bloodier and continue until 1939, the couple left Spain and went to Poland with their daughter, as Pack was appointed to the British Embassy of Warsaw in 1937.

## Becoming a Spy

They were not there long, however. Arthur suffered a stroke, and they had to leave immediately for Britain in order to get the best treatment for his full recovery. Amy had serious reasons for wanting to return to Warsaw, which she did while her husband was recovering.

In Warsaw, she had another affair with a young man named Edward Kulikowksi, who was acquainted with political circles there. Just after the Anschluss, the annexation of Austria by Germany, he told her that there was a prediction that the Nazi regime was about to lay its hands on Czechoslovakia. That wasn't unexpected. According to Amy's young lover and his sources, at least some in the Polish political establishment were not wanting to help Czechoslovakia, but instead, they were planning to seize a part of the country, themselves. This was shocking information and of course, that never happened. In any case, Amy gave that information to a British Secret Intelligence Service (SIS, commonly called MI6) agent she had come to know in Poland. His name was Jack Shelley. Shelley was impressed and thought a woman capable of obtaining information like this could be helpful to the agency. So, he suggested that she become a spy, which Amy accepted. We can imagine that this possibility excited her, given her adventurous character and her talent for seducing men. Reportedly, she was very popular with men, but women didn't like her much, and we are not surprised by that.

While the black clouds were gathering above Poland and Europe in 1938, in Warsaw, Amy had another affair with another young Pole with important political connections, probably even more important than the previous one. His name was Micah Lubienski, and he had many things to tell her during their romantic encounters, which she continuously passed onto Jack Shelley. She could have possibly passed the information about the Polish cryptologists breaking the German Enigma code we saw in Chapter 7 with Vera Atkins's story.

Amy was proving herself to be a talented and useful spy. However, her activities did not go down well with the Polish government. The Polish foreign minister was so annoyed that he immediately ordered her to exit Poland. Amy left the country in late September 1938. Around six months later, Arthur Pack was appointed again to the British Embassy in Chile, and they returned to Latin America on April 7, 1939. For Pack, returning to Chile was a return to his prestigious job position as well as a geographical return.

# A Sexpionage Master

Unlike Poland, the intelligence officers of the British Embassy in Santiago had a positive opinion of Amy's abilities. After Nazi Germany invaded Poland on September 1, 1939, they probably encouraged her to write articles against Hitler and the Nazis in newspapers in the country. The fact is that she wrote those articles, signing them with the name "Elizabeth Thomas," and that she became increasingly involved with the world of espionage.

During the following year, she distanced herself from her husband and became even closer to the intelligence world, first of all with a young American agent who worked for the Navy. His name was Paul Fairly, and he had to check how deep her collaboration with the intelligence agency would go. By now, it became clear that they had an affair, which was no surprise. The problem was that Amy became pregnant and they didn't keep the baby.

That wasn't a problem for the British intelligence, though, who were so convinced by her abilities and talents that they accepted her as a member of the British Security Coordination (BSC). This agency was part of MI6 and had very high levels of secrecy. Amy was obviously thrilled with this, so much so that she left her husband and their daughter behind and returned back to the United States after almost a decade. On November 25, 1940, she was in New York. Her boss in the BSC was Canadian spymaster William Stephenson, the "real James Bond" we've already met. They ordered her back to Washington, D.C., where she had previously lived. She was to find a hip house to live in and again enter the distinguished social scene of the capital.

Her mission had to do with the Lens-Lease Act, which was an act that supplied Allied nations, and in particular the British, the Soviets, the French, and the Chinese, with equipment and weapons, but also food and oil, in order to re-enforce their war efforts against the Axis powers. That may seem completely normal now, but it wasn't normal in the period that preceded March 11, 1941, the date it was signed into law. The United States did not enter the war before the Japanese attack at Pearl Harbor on December 7, 1941. There was strong opposition to having anything to do with it, as non-involvement was and still is very influential in the country because of its geography, which allows people to think there can't be any danger for them no matter what happens in the rest of the world. We can also see similar controversies in American politics and society regarding international wars today.

Part of the American leadership and President Roosevelt tried to pass a more active and assisting role of the US towards the United Kingdom and other nations that were fighting against the Axis. At the same time, somebody was very interested in helping the pro-assistance party get the policy through: the British themselves. So, the BSC targeted two senators who opposed the Lend-Lease Act and sent Amy to them to persuade them to change their minds. The two senators were Arthur Vandenberg and Thomas Connally. The latter proved to be immovable and unyielding, even under Amy's spells. However, Vandenberg indeed changed his mind and voted in favor of the act, helping it pass and become a policy. Of course, we don't know if Amy's efforts were a decisive factor in the senator's decision or what methods she used, but we like to think that the appeal of our seductive spy made a real difference in winning a lost case.

Apparently, the BSC believed that, too, since they immediately gave her a second mission in March 1941. This time, the target was the Italian Naval Attache in Washington, D.C., Admiral Alberto Lais. He was the man from whom the British could obtain the naval codes of the Italian Navy, strengthening their position against the Italians in the naval war in the Mediterranean Sea. Since the United States was not an aggressive participant yet, the Italian officer was still hanging around in Washington's lounges, the battlefield where Amy dominated. In that case, her past was helpful not only in her experience but in a more precise and direct way.

Admiral Lais was an old acquaintance of the early Amy Elizabeth Thorpe when she began charming older and distinguished gentlemen. Their relationship had been probably close and romantic but not yet sexual. In 1941, he was twice her age, but now she was much more dangerous. The Italian Admiral could not get to the point of giving away the codes himself, but he did the closest thing he could do without creating serious conscience problems for himself. He told her to approach a certain code clerk who worked in the Embassy of Italy. He could give her the codes. Amy indeed approached the employee, and this time, she used a different method. She faked being a journalist interested in naval codes, making him believe she wanted to write about him and his job. She did some interviews, and finally, she offered him some money, but not much. He accepted, and the Italian naval codes ended up in the hands of the British, giving them the opportunity to decode the messages of the Italian navy.

On March 27-29, the British navy won a decisive naval battle against the Italians near Cape Matapan or Tainaron in Peloponnese, Greece, the Battle of Cape Matapan. It is said that the codes obtained by Amy's operation were very helpful during that battle. We must add that Admiral Lais' heirs and the Italian defense ministry strongly opposed that story, even several decades later, refusing that he had collaborated in any way. According to yet another version, the Government Code and Cypher School broke the Italian codes. The fact is the Allies won the battle, and Amy had worked for that. The BSC were again delighted by her, and they gave her another mission right away, to prove it. And now the US intelligence, the Office of Strategic Services (OSS), has come to appreciate her abilities and hired her to work for them, too.

Amy's next mission was to find a way inside the Vichy France Embassy and get whatever information she could from there. She used again the fake journalist card, and she got a professional appointment with the press attaché of the embassy. Then, she did what she knew best: seducing him. It appears that, in this case, it was even easier for her because she really liked the guy. His name was Charles Emmanuel Brousse, and he had fought in WWI as an aviator with great success. In May 1941, he found it impossible to resist her, although he was possibly married, and their affair began.

A couple of months later, things became even better for Amy, as for some reason, the Vichy France Embassy was not happy with Brousse, and they downgraded his position in the embassy, cutting his salary in half. That was about enough for him, as, in fact, he was not happy in that Nazi-controlled state. Amy told him about the opportunity to collaborate with her: he would provide her with secret documents from the embassy and she would offer him a new salary. That was really a win-win situation.

But the best part of the story has yet to come, when the BSC gave Amy the mission to get the naval codes again, this time from Vichy France's navy. That meant Amy had to find a way inside the inner offices of the embassy since Brousse's job had nothing to do with the naval ciphers. She had to convince a guard to let her in. So, after trying for a while, she managed to create a friendly atmosphere with a guard, actually the night guard (that's important). That was in June 1942. Then, Amy and her lover, Brousse, made a bold move: they offered the night guard money if he let them in, telling him they fantasized about having sex in the empty embassy building by night. The guy took the money and obviously thought the whole thing was very entertaining, but just to be sure, they offered him a drink where they had added a drug. The guard fell asleep, and the satanic lovers rushed into the offices and found where the code books were. They also called a safecracker whom they had recruited earlier because the codebooks were kept in a safe. He opened the safe, and they had the books right in front of them. However, they didn't have enough time to take the books from the embassy, copy them, and bring them back without anyone noticing.

On June 24, 1942, Amy and Brousse followed a different plan. They again bribed the guard to let them in, as they wanted to have sex in the empty embassy. However, this time, they didn't drug him. Instead, they actually had sex inside the embassy, and when he came to check, he saw them nude and apologized. That was so convincing he would not come back for the rest of the night. Meanwhile, they had arranged for the safecracker to enter the embassy's building using a ladder, and he took the codebooks, had them photographed, and returned them while the guard thought the couple was just having a night of kinky passion.

The information obtained using this intriguing sexpionage story helped the Allies when they invaded North Africa in November 1942, giving them the opportunity to decode communications of Vichy France's navy. So, when years later, Amy was asked if she felt ashamed of her sexual methods, she responded like this: "Ashamed? Not in the least." And continued: "My superiors told me that the results of my work saved thousands of British and American lives…. It involved me in situations from which 'respectable' women draw back—but mine was total commitment. Wars are not won by respectable methods." (HistoryNet, 2006).

# Tragic Deaths Around a Stormy Life

Amy had played her part by using her seductive talents and contributed to the win in WWII with courage and resolve. After those important missions, she was considered way too exposed in the spy world to continue. Even the FBI had noticed her and put her under surveillance, even though the BSC and OSS informed the FBI she was working for them. It seems that the Military Intelligence Service was suspicious about her methods, too. So, although she wanted to return to France for a mission, her superiors kept her in Washington. She did, however, have a meeting with President Roosevelt which is worth mentioning. She talked with him for about an hour, telling him stories from her missions and her activities as a spy.

Amy eventually went to France right after it was liberated in 1944, and she lived there with Brousse. The couple got married after Amy's estranged husband, Arthur Pack, committed suicide in 1945. That was not the only tragedy that marked Amy's definitely not-so-harmonious family life. Her daughter lived in the United States and got married. Her son, whom she had left in Britain as a foster baby and was raised by a doctor and his wife, died fighting in the Korean War in the early 1950s. Amy died from cancer on December 1, 1963, aged 53. Her husband, Charles Brousse, died nine years later when a fire erupted in the medieval castle, they had lived in together in Castelnou.

# Chapter 10:

# Andrée Borrel—The Unseen

# Heroine

*One's philosophy is not best expressed in words; it is expressed in the choices one makes...and the choices we make are ultimately our responsibility.* –Eleanor Roosevelt

Andrée Borrel's background was more similar to that of Violette Szabo than Amy Elizabeth Thorpe. She came from a working-class family and was considered a tomboy instead of a seductive young lady. Both types of women had a role to play in the war effort. Yet, that doesn't mean Andrée wasn't beautiful. There can be many ways of being beautiful, and tomboys like herself and Violette, who are good at sports and adventurous, tend to have fantastic strong athletic bodies, confidence, and courage. They may not be fit for sexpionage in high diplomatic and military circles, but they can parachute and undertake dangerous missions and be active and decisive in the field. Andrée was like this, and she gave her life for the victory, too.

# A Working Young Ideologue Meets the French Resistance

Born on November 18, 1919, with the full name Andrée Raymonde Borrel, she was from a suburb in the north-western part of Paris. She was a tomboy and strong, according to her sister, so she loved to ride bicycles, hike, climb, and do whatever the boys did. Again, similarly to Violette Szabo, Andrée started working when she was only 14 years old. In her case, the most apparent reason was her father had died three years earlier, and she had to help maintain her family. Her first job was as a dress designer, and then she worked in a bakery and as a shop assistant in Paris after her family moved to the city.

Besides working, Andrée developed strong political and ideological convictions from a young age. Given her social status, she felt close to the socialist ideas that, in that period, had a high appeal in the European working classes. She was so involved that in 1939, she decided to go to Spain to fight with the Republicans against the Nationalists, as the Soviet Union and European socialists backed the Republicans, while Hitler and Mussolini backed General Franco's Nationalists. However, when the young French socialist arrived in Spain, she understood that the game was essentially over and the Nationalists had won, so she quickly left.

In October 1939, a month after World War II broke out, her family had to move again, this time to Toulon, because doctors had advised her mother to live in a warmer climate for her health. Nevertheless, politicized ideologue Andrée couldn't stay out of what was happening in the international politics arena. She completed a nursing course, and by the beginning of February 1940, she was working as a volunteer for the French branch of the Red Cross. She was transferred to a few different hospitals during the following months. Eventually, she ended up working at the Hôpital Compliméntaire when the Germans occupied Paris and France capitulated in June. The next month, the hospital closed.

One co-worker of Andrée, Lieutenant Maurice Dufour, proposed she enter a resistance group he was a member of called Pat Line. She accepted, and the job assigned to them by the organization was to establish a safe house on the coast near Perpignan, which is a city in southeastern France near the border with Spain. The safe house would be there for SOE agents, British pilots who were shot down, Jews, and anyone who tried to escape from occupied France. However, as the end of 1941 was approaching, the Gestapo breached the escape circuit that managed the safe house, and everybody who used it found themselves in great danger of being arrested. Andrée and Dufour had to flee the safe house in the area and the country itself, passing through the Pyrénées to Spain. That wasn't the end of the journey since Franco's Spain was not warring but an ally of Nazi Germany and Fascist Italy, so it was not the best place for members of the French Resistance to stay. They passed to neutral Portugal and from there to Great Britain. Andrée's flight landed in England on April 24, 1942.

# Agent of the British SOE

After her arrival, Andrée was brought to the Royal Patriotic School, which was the place where the internal security branch of British intelligence, called MI5, checked all those coming from continental Europe. Her interview was successful, as the agents believed her story was true and straightforward. They saw her as a perfect example of a bright, patriotic country girl who was not a security threat but a person who could enroll in the female branch of General De Gaulle's Free French Forces (FFF).

That's what Andrée hoped for, too. However, the FFF was not so open to it because the Pat Line she had worked with before fleeing France was an organization with networks that helped and collaborated with British agents and aviators who had been shot down. They insisted she had to tell them every detail about her activities there. Andrée was unwilling to do so, and her enrollment in the FFF never happened. Yet that didn't mean she would not fight for France in this war. The SOE had followed her case and decided that she could make a valuable agent, as she was exactly what they needed for a field agent. Interestingly, while she refused to report the details of the previous organization and her activities to the FFF, she had no problem sharing it with the SOE. So, the SOE approached her, and she accepted the position of a member of the British agency.

Like most of the ladies we have talked about in this book, Andrée became an agent of the SOE's F Section, officially a First Aid Nursing Yeomanry (FANY) member. Unlike some of them, she had great success during the training, and in the end, she was given the grade of lieutenant. The report said she was charming, intelligent, harsh, self-sufficient, and calm. On the other hand, she didn't have much imagination and organizational skills, but she functioned better following precise instructions. The report predicted that she could become a first-class agent for the SOE. For their part, the men who trained with her thought she was informal, playful, easy to like, and a scrappy lower-class girl who had remained innocent despite her involvement with the war.

## The First Woman to Land in France

We don't have to look for long to find something unique about Andrée's mission and landing in France: along with her partner in the mission, Lisa de Baissac, she was the first female SOE agent to land in the occupied country. That happened on September 25, 1942. Their code names were "Denise" for Andrée and "Odile" for Lisa. Their mission was to help the ongoing operation to create and establish resistance networks in Nazi-occupied Northern France, including Paris itself.

About a week later, at the beginning of October, Andrée was in the French capital, which she knew very well since she had lived there for several years. She was meeting Francis Suttill, who was the leader of the Prosper network we have already seen operating in Nazi-occupied Northern France. Her basic job would be that of the courier of the circuit. However, because of Suttill's poor French, Andrée was practically by his side all the time and devoted to his leadership, and she was the one who talked for him most of the time, pretending to be his sister. Another person who collaborated very closely with the two was Gilbert Norman, the wireless operator. After their initial meeting, they began their mission in Northern France and had great success during October and November when headquarters parachute dropped a large number of containers full of weapons. The drops of arms and material would be repeated several times during the following period.

Suttill was a married man and focused on his organizing job for the resistance network, but Andrée and Norman were young and free and had room for romance, too. They became lovers, and it was an intriguing relationship because they were from completely different social backgrounds: contrary to her working-class origins, he was wealthy and came from the upper social strata. Andrée broke not only the social class stereotypes but, with some other SOE agents, caused some mischief that the SOE headquarters didn't like too much, like playing cards in a café they fancied in Paris.

Nevertheless, her performance as an agent was amazing. Suttill was extremely enthusiastic about her, writing in a report in March 1943 that she was the best of the group, she shared the dangers and understood perfectly the security issues (probably he didn't know about the card games), and she was always calm; he concluded thanking them for having sent her to him.

## The Dismantling of Prosper Network

Unfortunately, Prosper network's happy days would not last much longer. Just the month after Suttill wrote that enthusiastic report about

Andrée, the Germans launched a devastating attack against the circuit. In fact, the preparation for its dismantling had begun several months earlier, during the period of its growth in November 1942. By then, a German agent had stolen an earlier raw list with names of people wanting to end the German occupation. Based on that list, the Sicherheitsdienst (SD) traced a significant part of the Prosper network by observing them for a few months without intervening. As Prosper grew with local recruits and agents coming from Britain, many more people were falling under the surveillance of German intelligence.

In April 1943, the SD was ready to launch a large-scale operation to damage and dismantle Prosper. Suttill, Norman, and Andrée Borrell were arrested, and many other members of the SOE and French Resistance, who counted in the hundreds, followed. Initially, Andrée was prisoned in the Fresnes Prison, where the Germans attempted to interrogate her, but she was so silent and contemptuous that they stopped trying. She also found a sneaky way to send messages to her mother. She was still confident and reassuring, asked for things like notebooks, and sent many sweet kisses.

After a year or so, on May 13, 1944, Andrée and six more imprisoned women of the SOE F Section, including our known Sonia Olschanezky, were transferred to the SD headquarters in Paris and from there to the prison of Karlsruhe. That was preferable to a concentration camp, and the conditions for the prisoners were much better and milder than those we've seen in previous cases. Furthermore, as the war was becoming positive for the Allies and negative for the Nazis, this created a good mood among the prisoners, as hope that the Allied forces would sooner or later liberate them was growing. Allied raids on German soil were becoming more common, and each of them was a reason for joy for Andrée and the other SOE and resistance members, even though they could end up being hit in these raids.

# Nazi Horror

Andrée and the other women with her initially were not put in a concentration camp, but an even worse destiny awaited them. On July 6, 1944, Andrée, Sonia Olschanezky, and two more women, named Vera Leigh and Diana Rowden, were transferred to the Natzweiler-Struthof concentration camp, which was located between the two villages in Gau Baden-Alsace, in the occupied French territories. The order was that they should be executed as soon as possible.

Their presence in the camp and the execution order was strange to both the guards and prisoners, as the other prisoners were male, and it was obvious that the four women hadn't previously been in a concentration camp, as they looked in better shape than the typical concentration camp prisoners. That night, they were divided and put in separate cells, yet they found a way to communicate with other detainees. One of them, the Belgian Dr. Georges Boogaerts, offered Andrée some cigarettes, and she passed him some money she had inside a pouch of tobacco. One other prisoner, a physician of the Belgian army, Albert Guérisse, recognized Andrée as he was the leader of the Pat O'Leary Line's branch in Marseille, and they had worked together during her time as a member of that organization, and he talked briefly with one of the other women. Then, the guards guided them into a building, and the Nazi horror began.

That building was where the crematorium was. They brought the four women in there, one after another, every couple of minutes. In there, they ordered them to undress, and then they injected them, telling them it was a vaccine for typhus when, in reality, it was a lethal poison, phenol. Right after the injection, the woman became unconscious and was put in the crematorium to burn. The last woman, we don't know if she was Andrée, unexpectedly returned to her senses despite the injection while they were dragging her into the crematorium. She put up a fierce fight, and she deeply scratched the face of the camp executioner named Peter Straub. The guards pushed her into the oven while she was alive and conscious.

Those responsible for these horrendous executions were among the Nazi war criminals who were convicted after the war. The camp doctor received the death penalty.

# Honors

Andrée was awarded posthumously the *Croix de Guerre* from the French Republic after the war and the *Médaille de la Résistance*. The British honored her with the King's Commendation for Brave Conduct. She is one of the SOE agents mentioned in the Valençay SOE Memorial and in the SOE Agents Memorial in Westminster, London. Her name is also mentioned in the Tempsford Memorial in Bedfordshire, which is in England. A poignant watercolor that hangs in the Special Forces Club in London pictures herself and the other three women who were executed in the crematorium of Natzweiler-Struthof. It was created by painter Brian Stonehouse, who was an SOE agent, too, and was one of the witnesses of the four women's final moments.

# Conclusion:

# The Legacy of Female Secret

# Agents in World War II

*Never in the field of human conflict was so much owed by so many to so few.* —
Winston Churchill

In this book, we have talked about nine of the most important and famous women who contributed to the Allies' victory in the Second World War as agents and spies. They were different women from various backgrounds, some being poorer and from lower social classes and others wealthier with higher status. Nevertheless, all had a common passion and determination to fight for their countries and freedom.

We highlighted the stories of Nancy Wake, Virginia Hall, Noor Inayat Khan, Pearl Witherington, Krystyna Skarbek, Vera Atkins, Violette Szabo, Amy Elizabeth Thorpe, and Andree Borrel. Nancy Wake was an independent woman with resilience and courage, capable of escaping capture and adapting to new roles. Virginia Hall was a strategic mind and tenacious woman who pursued active roles in diplomacy and war despite her personal circumstances. Noor Inayat Khan was a sensitive and pacifist storyteller who decided that the Allied cause was just to enter the battleground and give her life supporting it. Pearl Witherington, the only woman to lead a network of the SOE, displayed determination, resilience, and organizational skills. Krystyna Skarbek demonstrated adaptability and courage in the face of aversions and transformations, and her life would make a great tragedy. Vera Atkins was a woman of strength and commitment to justice, a figure of guidance and support. Violette Szabo was an adventurous, courageous, and tenacious young woman who sacrificed her life for victory. Amy Elizabeth Thorpe, a seductive and influential woman with connections to political and military environments, gained crucial intelligence. Andree Borrel was a real patriot who faced arrest and imprisonment by the Gestapo but maintained fortitude and bravery until her execution.

It's important to remember that all those women, actually most often young girls, entered the war and risked or gave their lives as volunteers. None of them had to put themselves in that position. None of them were forced to do so. Neither did they gain professionally or financially. The sacrifice was as authentic and pure as it could be, also because, as females, there was no political, legal, or moral imperative for them to actively join the war effort. Many times, they didn't even have time for proper and complete training, as the urgent need for more agents was so pressing that it didn't leave many choices for the people who had to make the hard decisions.

Each of those women had a distinct personality, dreams, and goals, and almost all of them had nothing to do with the military and war previously. They weren't violent, aggressive, or hostile. They were independent spirits seeking high adventure and intrigue, though, and we can imagine that if war hadn't come upon Europe and the world in 1939, these ladies would have found other ways to express their dynamic and proud characters and inclinations. Unlike beliefs that think peace comes from passive and "safe" attitudes, the nine female agents and warriors we met in this book show us that it takes high spirit, deep-rooted values, and courage to face the aggressors and secure freedom and justice, without which, peace would mean only submission and slavery. We can describe it with a word that isn't used much these days: heroism.

The stories of our nine ladies can help us also understand that victory in war and freedom, or the very survival of a nation, depends not only on the massive battles but extends to less obvious places where covert operations and obtaining information can have a crucial role. Furthermore, it comes from the collective efforts of societies determined to resist and fight and individuals committed to a cause larger than themselves and who are capable of inspiring others.

We have to remember that our nine female agents and spies represent many more women, thousands more, who similarly joined the war effort and offered their service from any standpoint they could, helping, risking, and many times giving their lives. We mentioned a few, and many more deserve to be mentioned. The legacy of all those extraordinary women not only proves that bravery, integrity, and heroism know no gender and that women can be perfectly capable and daring even in the darkest times and situations. It also underscores that life's unpredictability can bring us extraordinary challenges and unprecedented circumstances that we must be ready to meet.

Stories like the ones we've seen in this book emphasize the vast importance of individual responsibility and faith in our capacity to shape the course of history. We need to fight for our societies and our way of life instead of taking it for granted and adopting passive or naive ideals. All those women who actively volunteered to support their societies in their harsher struggles did not stay home imagining or wishing for peace. They profoundly understood, in the moment, how critical it was to fight for freedom, and that was a collective endeavor. They acted as free, responsible, and courageous individuals, embracing their unique abilities and strengths.

*Thank you so much for reading my*
*book about these courageous women,*
*who made such a huge contribution to the*
*outcome of World War II and the world.*


*There are 3 more books coming in this series,*
*telling the stories of similar amazing women.*


*All their stories need to be told.*


*If you have enjoyed reading my book,*
*I would be very grateful if you would*
*have time to leave a review for me.*

https://mybook.to/O51r


*Thanks so much*
*Nel Mead*


*http://booksformeandmine.com*

# References

*Activity report of Virginia Hall (Diane)*. (1944). Saint-Heckler circuit reports, F Section. https://web.archive.org/web/20210225140037/http://www.8 01492.org/Air%20Crew/Ewart/Saint-Heckler%20Reports.pdf

Agence France-Presse. (2012, November 12). *Muslim "spy princess" honoured in London*. https://web.archive.org/web/20170906180554/https://www. aquila-style.com/focus-points/muslim-spy-princess/23662/

Andrews, A. (n.d.). *Archie Andrews quotes*. Goodreads. https://www.goodreads.com/quotes/294735-never-underestimate-the-power-of-a-woman

Atwood, K. J. (2013). *Women heroes of World War II: 26 stories of espionage, sabotage, resistance, and rescue*. 1st ed. Women of Action. Chicago: Chicago Review Press.

BBC News Online. (2008, April 1). *War heroine not classed leader*. http://news.bbc.co.uk/2/hi/uk_news/7323747.stm

BBC News. (2006, April 11). *War heroine honoured 63 years on*. http://news.bbc.co.uk/2/hi/uk_news/4898302.stm

BBC History. (2011, July 22). *Noor Inayat Khan*. https://www.bbc.co.uk/history/historic_figures/inayat_khan_ noor.shtml

Bernstein, A. (2011, August 9). Nancy Wake, 'White Mouse' of World War II, dies at 98. *Washington Post*.

Blum, H. (2016). *The last goodnight: A World War II story of espionage, adventure, and betrayal*. HarperCollins.

Boyd, W. (2018, February 22). *The secret persuaders*. The Guardian. https://www.theguardian.com/uk/2006/aug/19/military.seco ndworldwar

Central Intelligence Agency. (n.d.) *The people of the CIA... making an impact: Virginia Hall.* https://web.archive.org/web/20080311225315/https://www. cia.gov/news-information/featured-story-archive/2007-featured-story-archive/the-people-of-the-cia.html

Churchill, W. (n.d.). *Winston Churchill quotes*. BrainyQuote. https://www.brainyquote.com/quotes/winston_churchill_100 790

Davenport-Hines, R. (2019, March 22). *A woman of no importance by Sonia Purnell review — Virginia Hall, the one-legged female spy who beat the Gestapo.* The Times. https://www.thetimes.co.uk/article/a-woman-of-no-importance-by-sonia-purnell-review-virginia-hall-the-one-legged-female-spy-who-beat-the-gestapo-3js8vwhfm

Encyclopedia of World Biography. (n.d.). *Christine Granville Biography*. https://www.notablebiographies.com/supp/Supplement-Fl-Ka/Granville-Christine.html

Faulder, L. (2020, February 10). Review: the invisible, agents of ungentlemanly warfare challenges stereotypes about women and war. *Edmonton Journal.* https://edmontonjournal.com/entertainment/local-arts/review-the-invisible-agents-of-ungentlemanly-warfare-challenges-stereotypes-about-women-and-war

FitzSimons, P. (2011). *Nancy Wake: A biography of our greatest war heroine 1912-2011.* Revised edition. HarperCollins Publishers.

Gates, M. (n.d.). *Melinda Gates quotes.* Quotefancy. https://quotefancy.com/quote/1202221/Melinda-Gates-A-woman-with-a-voice-is-by-definition-a-strong-woman-But-the-search-to-find

Gilbert, A. (2023, October 16). *Battles of El-Alamein | WWII turning point, British victory.* Encyclopedia Britannica. https://www.britannica.com/event/battles-of-El-Alamein

Helm, Sarah (2015). *If this is a woman; inside Ravensbrück, Hitler's concentration camp for women.* Little, Brown.

HistoryNet Staff (2006, December 6). *Amy Elizabeth Thorpe: WWII's Mata Hari.* HistoryNet. https://www.historynet.com/amy-elizabeth-thorpe-wwiis-mata-hari/

Leafe, D. (2012, October 16). *The spy who loved men: she was Churchill's favourite spy, the inspiration for Bond's lover in Casino.* Daily Mail Online. https://www.dailymail.co.uk/news/article-2213623/The-spy-loved-men-She-Churchills-favourite-spy-inspiration-Bonds-lover-Casino-Royale-knife-strapped-thigh.html

Leech, G. (2011, August 9). *Fearless matriarch of resistance.* The Australian.

Lichfield, J. (2011, August 8). *Resistance heroine who led 7,000 men against the Nazis.* The Independent. https://www.independent.co.uk/news/world/europe/resistance-heroine-who-led-7-000-men-against-the-nazis-2334156.html

Macdonald, B. (2001). *The true intrepid: Sir William Stephenson and the unknown agents.* Raincoast.

Mandela, N. (n.d.). *Nelson Mandela quotes.* Goodreads. https://www.goodreads.com/quotes/5156-i-learned-that-courage-was-not-the-absence-of-fear

Marks, L. (n.d.). *Leo Marks quotes.* Goodreads. https://www.goodreads.com/quotes/9771679-there-were-only-three-things-which-soe-s-agents-could-anticipate

Marley, B. (n.d.). *Bob Marley quotes.* Quotefancy. https://quotefancy.com/quote/35454/Bob-Marley-You-never-know-how-strong-you-are-until-being-strong-is-your-only-choice

Milton, G. (2017). *Churchill's ministry of ungentlemanly warfare*. Picador.

Morpurgo, M. (2019, May 30). *Michael Morpurgo remembers his heroic uncle, Francis Cammaerts.* The Telegraph. https://www.telegraph.co.uk/men/thinking-man/michael-morpurgo-remembers-heroic-uncle-francis-cammaerts/

Mulley, C. (n.d.). *Christine Granville quotes.* Goodreads. https://www.goodreads.com/quotes/tag/christine-granville

Myre, G. (2019, April 18). *"A woman of no importance" finally gets her due.* NPR. https://www.npr.org/2019/04/18/711356336/a-woman-of-no-importance-finally-gets-her-due

Mulley, Clare (2012). *The spy who loved: The secrets and lives of Christine Granville, Britain's first female special agent of the Second World War.* Macmillan.

*Noor Anayat Khan: The Princess who became a spy.* (2006, February 20). The Independent. https://www.independent.co.uk/arts-entertainment/books/features/noor-anayat-khan-the-princess-who-became-a-spy-6108704.html

O'Conner, Bernard (2014). *Churchill's angels.* Stroud. Amberley Publishing.

Pallister, D. (2017, November 26). *Sharpshooter, paratrooper, hero: The woman who set France ablaze.* The Guardian. https://www.theguardian.com/uk/2008/apr/01/nationalarchives.secondworldwar

*Pearl Witherington.* (n.d.). Spartacus Educational. https://www.spartacus-educational.com/SOEwitherington.htm

Perrin, N. (n.d.). *SOE agent profiles. Christine Granville.* Nigel Perin. https://nigelperrin.com/christinegranville.htm

Pygas, M. (2013, September 5). *10 Amazing female spies who brought down the Nazis.* Listverse. https://listverse.com/2013/09/05/10-women-spies-who-brought-down-the-third-reich/

Radmacher, M. A. (n.d.). *Mary Anne Radmacher quotes.* Goodreads. https://www.goodreads.com/author/quotes/149829.Mary_Anne_Radmacher

Roosevelt, E. (n.d.). *Eleanor Roosevelt quotes.* Goodreads. https://www.goodreads.com/quotes/202842-one-s-philosophy-is-not-best-expressed-in-words-it-is

Rose, S. (2020). *D-Day girls.* Broadway Books

Russell, S. (2017, September 21). *Nancy Wake - they called her the "White Mouse - incredible Allied SOE agent of World War Two.* War History Online. https://www.warhistoryonline.com/world-war-ii/mouse-threatened-germans-france.html

Hildreth, R. (1988, May 29). *Cynthia, a Minnesota patriot with brains, beauty and guts.* Star Tribune. https://www.newspapers.com/image/195324871/?terms=%22Amy%20Elizabeth%20Thorpe%22&match=1&clipping_id=120365715

Stevenson, William (November 2006). *Spymistress: The life of Vera Atkins, the greatest female secret agent of World War II.* Arcade Publishing.

Stroud, Rick (2017). *Lonely Courage: The true story of the SOE heroines who fought to free Nazi-Occupied France.* Simon & Schuster.

The Telegraph. (2009, September 30). *Captain Les Fernandez.* https://www.telegraph.co.uk/news/obituaries/military-obituaries/army-obituaries/6248212/Captain-Les-Fernandez.html

Trueman, C. N. (2015, May 18). *Special Operations Executive.* History Learning Site. https://www.historylearningsite.co.uk/world-war-two/resistance-movements/special-operations-executive/

U.S. Department of Defense. (2016, March 2). *WASPs were pioneers for female pilots of today, tomorrow.* https://web.archive.org/web/20190118025148/https://dod.defense.gov/News/Article/Article/684700/wasps-were-pioneers-for-female-pilots-of-today-tomorrow/

Vigurs, Kate (2021). *Mission France: The true history of the women of SOE*. Yale University Press.

Violette Szabó GC Museum. (n.d). *Violette Szabo. George Cross and Croix de Guerre*. http://violetteszabomuseum.org.uk/history

Ward, P.S. (2000, April 19). *Nancy Wake, the white mouse*. NZEDGE. http://www.nzedge.com/legends/warriors/nancy-wake/

Wilder, U. M. (2017, June). The psychology of espionage. *Studies in Intelligence. 1*(2).

# Image References

Made in the USA
Thornton, CO
05/27/24 14:48:40

1a37d6d5-79bb-4f46-a29e-9deb95ec0a45R01